Painters Who Fucking
Know How to Paint

I0494561

Opening Reception
Thursday, June 7 2018, 6-9pm

Gallery Exhibition
June 7, 2018 - July 14, 2018

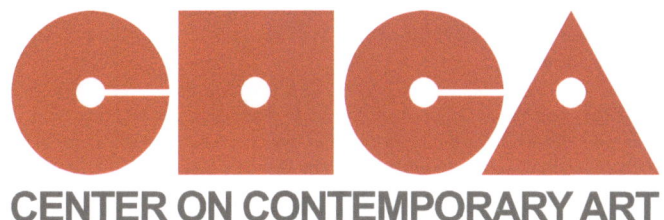

CENTER ON CONTEMPORARY ART

Catalog & Show Credits

CoCA

Published May 2018 by:

Center on Contemporary Art
114 Third Avenue South
Seattle, WA 98104
http://www.cocaseattle.org
info@cocaseattle.org
206 728-1980
Copyright ©2018 Center on Contemporary Art
ISBN: 978-0-9990819-5-2

Curators:

Kate Vrijmoet
Kate Sweeney

Catalog:

Ray C. Freeman III

Cover Art:

Ken Kelly (front), Paula Whelan (back)

Artists' images and texts used by permission. The artist statements and bios in this catalog have been lightly edited, primarily for length, to fit on the page.

All rights reserved. No part of this book may be reproduced in any manner whatsoever without written permission except in the case of brief quotations embodied in critical articles and reviews.

Board of Directors:

Eddie Reed, *President, Acting Treasurer*
Judith Rayl, *Chair*
Archis Gore, *Secretary*
Joseph Bisacca
Sara Everett
Travis Monroe
Joseph Roberts
Joy Turner
Kayleigh Wold
Harmony Wolfe

CoCA Staff:

Nichole DeMent, *Executive and Artistic Director*

Board of Advisors:

Ray C. Freeman III, CoCA *Publisher*
David Francis, PhD, *Curator at Large*
Anna R. Hurwitz, CoCA *Archives Project Director*
Miguel Edwards, *Previous Board President*

Special Thanks:

Elysian Brewing
4Culture
Individual Donors
CoCA Members

 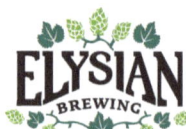

Table of Contents

Notes on *Painters Who Fucking Know How to Paint*

Kate Sweeney, co-curator

Hoping to stimulate a reaction to the question 'Is painting still relevant?', we chose painters for this show whose work delivers an emphatically positive response.

These artists each create in a demonstrably present moment, mounting an investigation into the world today. Their narrative concerns explore current political structures, the environment, and the state of our strained social fabric. Their expeditions into process look to extend the definition of painting itself. Their unique perceptual forays stimulate new realizations in the viewer.

The selected work emphasizes the personal dialog that the painter has with the surface in front of them, whether they approach their ends from **perceptual concerns**, creating visual phenomena/effects on a surface; **narrative concerns**, addressing emotional, political and social subjects; or **process concerns**, investigating what can constitute a painting through materials and methods explorations. Each artist blends and transmutes each of these concerns into a work that describes a universe of their own making, a trip into new lands for the viewer.

These organizational principles are guideposts for the journey through the show, a way to navigate the work for the viewer.

The *perceptual* approach can be defined as a response to retinal/visual stimulation, the creation of a gestalt or sense of a unified whole using shapes or constructs evocative of form, space, and light. This approach can play with 2D/3D space creation on a surface, impart physical color sensations, and through composition and design provide the sensation of energy, movement, action, and reification. Observation and aesthetics combine into a whole.

The *narrative* approach allows the subject/content to drive the structure.

Historical, political, topical, fantastical, social, emotional, psychological, temporal and symbolic scenes are constructed on the surface and serve as a window into a new world. A formative idea of what the painting is trying to explicate drives the execution. A narrative can also be built post hoc, as meaning is derived from the record of marks and process.

The *process* approach relates to the physical act of creating, and is a response to the material surface. The action required for getting elements onto a substrate drives the structure: gesture, reaction, movement. Material choices of surface and media provide a tactility and sensuousness that prompts a physical reaction, and a means for exploring what a 'painting' is. Shading into 'objectness' and sculpture, the 'thingness' of a painting at times supersedes any illusory space within the frame.

Developing a unique vocabulary of marks, shapes, images, and colors that drives a cohesive personal image forward, every artist sets parameters for their choices, whether intentionally or unconsciously, which lead to a new visual language. These unspoken rules drive the object to a resolution that positions it within the artist's own aesthetic world.

Artists can also work from a point of *reaction* and/or *conception*: gestural reaction vs planned approach, observation vs idea-driven intellectual plans. They may set up a plan or concept and then react to the work in progress from a perceptual stance, creating a cascading series of decisions that lead to a unexpected result, a 'call and response' dialogue with the work.

A philosophical intent, as it pertains to the motive behind the act of painting, be it observational, political, social, emotional or metaphysical, also drives the act of making.

Combining these approaches leads to abstract emotional maps, figurative

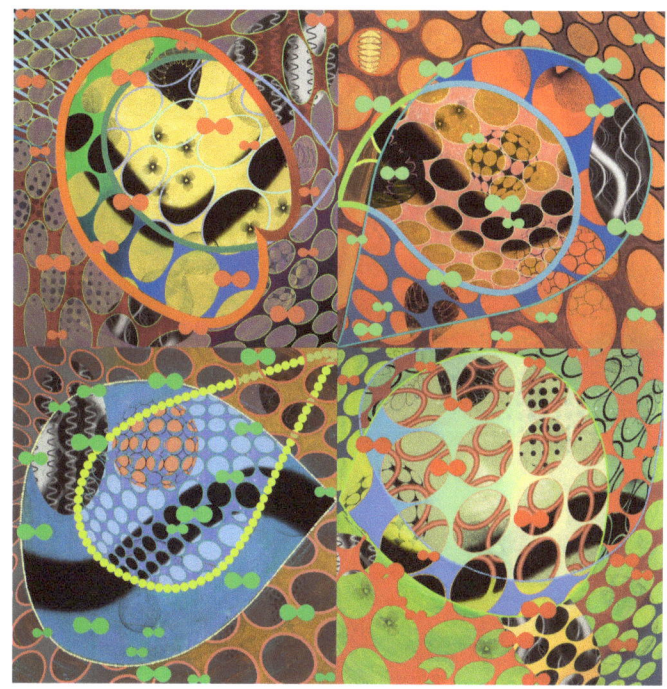

Crazy Quilt
Oil acrylic ink, paper, and transfer on panel, 72 x 72", 2015

temporal records, emotional symbolic scenes, gestural landscapes and fantasy political still-lifes.

Laura Hamje, in her observational, perceptual, process-driven record of natural phenomena, records a sensation of light captured in a single moment, thereby creating an emotional narrative. Adrianne Smits' perceptual approach goes through a symbolic, narrative filter to create a view into a magical world. Cable Griffith uses perceptual cues combined with a strong vocabulary of mark-making to build his kingdoms.

Kathy Liao, Alex Kanevsky, Jennifer Pochinski, Susanna Bluhm, Kathy Gore Fuss, Marie Gagnon, Karen Kaapke, and Ruthi V. use a strong observational stance to record perceptions that suggest an emotional narrative, a response to the moment they are recording.

Brian Cypher uses process to create meaning — an action painting conversational record. Jazz Brown uses a vocabulary of geometries and reification to explore metaphysical ideas of unity and separation.

Carole d'Inverno, Robert Hardgrave, Allan Packer and David Hytone all use a well-developed vocabulary of marks and colors to create a historical, political or social narrative anchored in process. Patricia Hagen and Natalie Niblack use a narrative, emotional approach to shape their perceptual response to nature. Ron Hall reveals ideas and narratives in scenes and portraits that access and instigate emotional responses.

Margie Livingston employs her process to create and record an emotional narrative driven by her use of materials. Ken Kelly is all process, creating objects that exist on their own terms. Flora Ramirez Bustamante and Paula Whelan have a call and response with their process, creating a record of reactions and investigations.

At an interesting point in our civilization, with many old ideas and preconceived notions flying to bits, how an artist navigates the landscape of our humanness gives us a scouting party for the way forward. The participating artists offer the viewer worlds and journeys, access into their investigations of what a painting can be, now and in the future.

Combining all the structural and procedural elements and approaches, as these artists do, provides a hearty yes to the initial question. This rich output from the group is a new world to mine and explore, argue with, and marvel at.

What does it mean to really fucking paint?

Kate Vrijmoet, co-curator

Since the late 1960s and the coming of post-painterly abstraction, has painting been *dead*, as some then claimed — or just on life support? And, even if someone can really fucking paint — is it important? Dare we, in this show, take back for painting the wide cultural significance that it had in the Postwar era?

Perhaps we don't need to, especially if painting has actually been the presence in the room with the greatest staying power all along. One premise of this show is that painting is vigorous, diverse, and burgeoning despite half a century of solemn attempts to trivialize it. Not being a trend but a vital human activity, it just won't die. So we look at artists who can really fucking paint not in a valedictory spirit, as if they were the last of their kind rallying one more time, but to recognize that they are pushing the art form forward. There will be artists in the future who can really fucking paint, too. And they will know these painters as creators and torch bearers, not stragglers defending their tiny hill.

Just before painting was considered to have died, it was also considered among the most macho things to do, hand in glove with drinking bouts, motorcycle accidents, and abandoning wives and children. When did it tend in a ladylike or at least female direction? About the time it died? The enormous Postwar wave of women who painted seriously may, in certain circles, have been seen as a symptom of the failure of the form, so that in examining the vitality of painting, perhaps it's good to look at the gendered make-up of the party. Whether women were welcome to take their places only in a supposedly declining field is outside the scope of this essay, but it's a thought to think for the time it takes to think it.

Once upon a time, we were taught that the most painterly painting was brushy, in the tradition of Rubens, Velasquez, Delacroix and Sargent. It was not finicky, in the way of Van Der Weyden, Poussin, Ingres and Dali.

The most painterly painting was rapid-looking and inconceivably sure-handed, whereas the painting with the highest finish looked slow and meticulous and difficult. Art historians were fond of this stylistic dichotomy transcending bigger movements, but do we need that thinking now? Do we look at style to determine who can really fucking paint? Or are we looking for connection and emotional engagement? Perhaps the brush, however a painter wields it, is a tool of engagement. This show will give people an opportunity to test that thesis.

Perhaps it is simply human nature to praise one thing at the expense of another, to praise it not only for being what it is but for not being what it is not. Is that our most useful lens, or does it only cloud over the main task — finding artists who can really fucking paint? We have found 24 of them, and they are as various and contrasting as can be imagined. Looking at their work is an object lesson in how to contrast without typing or restricting.

I want to ask viewers and readers to try out the idea that even the most cerebral painting engages us emotionally. Its physicality is a form of touch, brushing against our minds, confronting our bodies. Professor Gyorgy Kepes wrote of painting as a skin, on the most fragile of supports, and he believed this was a secret of its lastingness. It's like us, and we too persist. Can we look at a painting as a brother, a sister, a mother…? If so, then we will experience the deepest of emotions, and a shift in our haptic sense.

The artists in this show were chosen for many reasons, but one thing their work has in common is its ability to reach out. Not to linger and wait for you to come on over. Consider Brian Cypher, in *Fatal Flower*: it scintillates and embraces you. His *Buried Under Branches and Blues* suggests the death of the heart, the physical heart. Is Susanna Bluhm, in *Snow on*

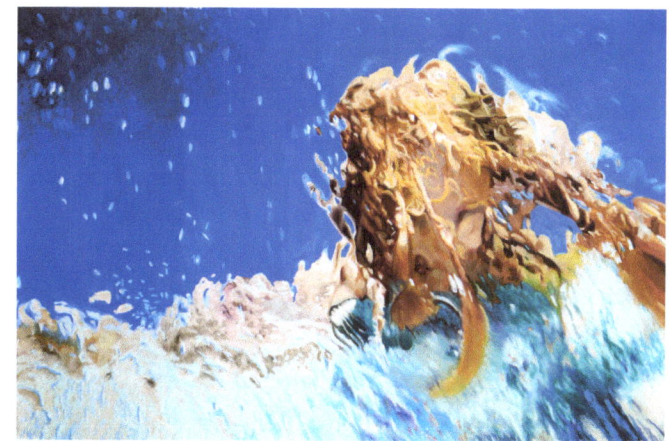

What you get is to be changed.
More and more by each glistening minute.
Oil on canvas, 80 x 125", 2012

Cindy's Hair Puffs, making a throne of ice for us to confront ourselves from? It's important to remember that a painter can rearrange the weather for us – that too is physical touch. In *I Call This Home*, Kathy Gore Fuss literally pulls us in through deep perspective with impressive obstacles. In Timber, she weds immense forest floor activity with a unique aural hush, and we need to hear this painting.

At first, the works of Flora Ramirez Bustamente, Cable Griffith, and Jazz Brown bear no particular resemblance to one another. But we need to pay attention to how much is happening in each, at the very surface, without deep space implied. These works come as close to us as any in the show, either luminescing into our own space, or sharing it with us, right at eye level

And what of nostalgia? That most crushing of emotions, the one we may not want to admit we're subject to, because it is just too kitschy. Not here. The works of Laura Hamje, Jennifer Pochinski, and Robert Hargrave are deeply nostalgic – landscapes as a child might recall them from the back seat of a car, or from a trip to the Riviera in the late 1950s, or from a nook in the corner of a cabaret. These are not the artists' intentions, you say? Not their subjects? This raises a crucial point – is it up to you to catch the meaning of the artist, or to find what is deeply personal to you in a painting, regardless of the artist's intentions? In every important interaction in life, we do more than we intend, we control less than we aim to.

There is figuration galore in the show, in its most intimate form, the self-portrait. Kathy Liao testifies before eternity that this is who she is and what she looks like. She shows us privacy, not pomp. Karen Kaapcke does the same in fantastically elegant, Klimtian expressions, and Ron Hall shows us that nothing is more revealing than a mask, barely covering a face full of confrontation. The distance each artist sets is instructive – the most

disguised face is the nearest to us.

Sometimes, painting goes iconic. And I wonder if the types of icons are more important than the fact of iconic painting. Ruthie V. gives us *Venus* – she's not kidding around. Adrianne Smits: a holy compound in a forest, one of the oldest tropes on earth. Margie Livingston references a keynote of classical painting and sculpture – the shapely drapery – without suggesting anything at all is draped. How far is the iconic from the apocalyptic? Not very, perhaps, and we should be strong enough to look at both. Paula Whelan's *Indecisive* looks threatening and joyous at once, but Natalie Niblack gets down to business in a different way, working a Flemish Hell into our lives.

Allan Packer, Alex Kanevsky, David Hytone, and Patricia Hagen take us back to the early 1960s to ask us to look at a crevasse in the earth, the detritus of our parents, a roomful of doors, a landscape in the snow. Meanings different than they once were, for we live under far greater threat than we did 60 years ago – climate change, seismic activity frighteningly understood, the failure of privacy, have all changed our lives.

Ken Kelly, Marie Gagnon, and Carole d'Inverno also reference another era with their paintings, one in which formal beauty seduced – brushiness, composition, abstract vistas. Yet their paintings could belong only to now, and that is a matter of mood and meaning.

So – seduction. Is that a proper aim of fucking good painting? Of course it is. A painter asks that you come naked and vulnerable to the work, laden not with information but with curiosity and a sense of possibility. How else are you to connect? What greater readiness can you bring?

> **"An individual painting can become a new place in itself, with sensations of things that might happen in a place, such as weather, touch, landscape, temperature, sex or noise. Abstract marks interact with more recognizable shapes, and a kind of narrative ensues."**

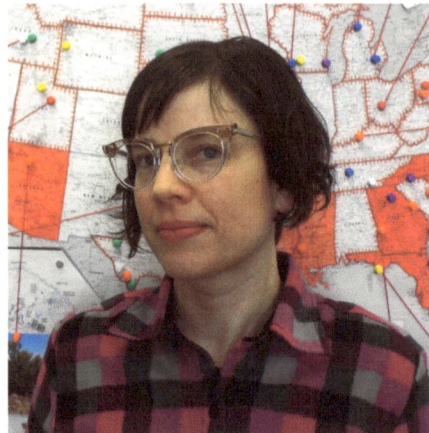

Susanna Bluhm

Susanna Bluhm is a Seattle-based artist whose work has been shown in solo exhibitions nationally and internationally. She earned her BA in Studio Art from California State University Humboldt and her MFA from the University of Illinois at Urbana-Champaign. In 2005 Susanna was an artist-in-residence at the Irish Museum of Modern in Dublin and at the Karl Hofer Gesellschaft in Berlin. She was a member of SOIL artist-run gallery in Seattle for five years, and is currently represented by G. Gibson Gallery in Seattle. In 2012 she was awarded an Artist Trust Grant for Artist Projects, and in 2014 she was the recipient of the Behnke Foundation's Neddy Artist Award in Painting. Her work has been featured in Art in America, and has been included three times in the publication New American Paintings. Bluhm's paintings are included in the collections of Daimler Contemporary (Berlin), Microsoft Corporation, Capital One, The Allen Institute, Swedish Medical Center and the City of Seattle. Originally from Los Angeles, Susanna lives in Seattle with her wife and son.

My paintings are usually related in some way to my physical environments and experience of them. Also, they are experiments in creating new environments. An individual painting can become a new place in itself, with sensations of things that might happen in a place, such as weather, touch, landscape, temperature, sex or noise. Abstract marks interact with more recognizable shapes, and a kind of narrative ensues.

The paintings submitted for CoCA's exhibition *Painters Who Fucking Know How to Paint* are from a series called The March Snow of New York.

The basic compositions of the paintings are based on photos I took in New York City in March of 2015. It snowed a lot, and after their long winter the New Yorkers were not excited about the snow, but I was. Snow, and weather, can be a story about sensory experience, cultural expectations, nostalgia, and disappointment. I like to think about the story of the weather referenced in the painting and also of the weather in the painting itself. The snow in the painting can also just be paint, or even frosting one might want to lick.

Semi-abstract "characters" show up in the paintings and suggest meanings with their repetition and associations with each other. Among these is a chunk of green and white stripes, which come from the green and white striped pajama bottoms from Suzanne Valadon's The Blue Room, 1923. To me, this character is a queer, feminist reclaiming of the history of painting. Also featured are Black Cindy's hair puffs (representative of her character on the TV show Orange is the New Black), and the Hebrew letter Bet (because Cindy and I both converted to Judaism). A pink fir tree is an odd, out-of-place Pacific Northwestern interloper and solo eloper in the big city.

Making these semi-abstract landscape-based paintings with a personal narrative running underneath is a three-pronged effort. I am looking at my agency in the landscape. I am trying to spend more time in the place by painting it. I'm using paint to make physical contact again. In this intimate way, the paintings explore landscape as a lover and loved one, enmeshed with the paint, and without the safe distance usually afforded by the Sublime in traditional Western landscape painting.

Snow on Cindy's Hair Puffs
Oil and acrylic on canvas, 40 x 40", 2016

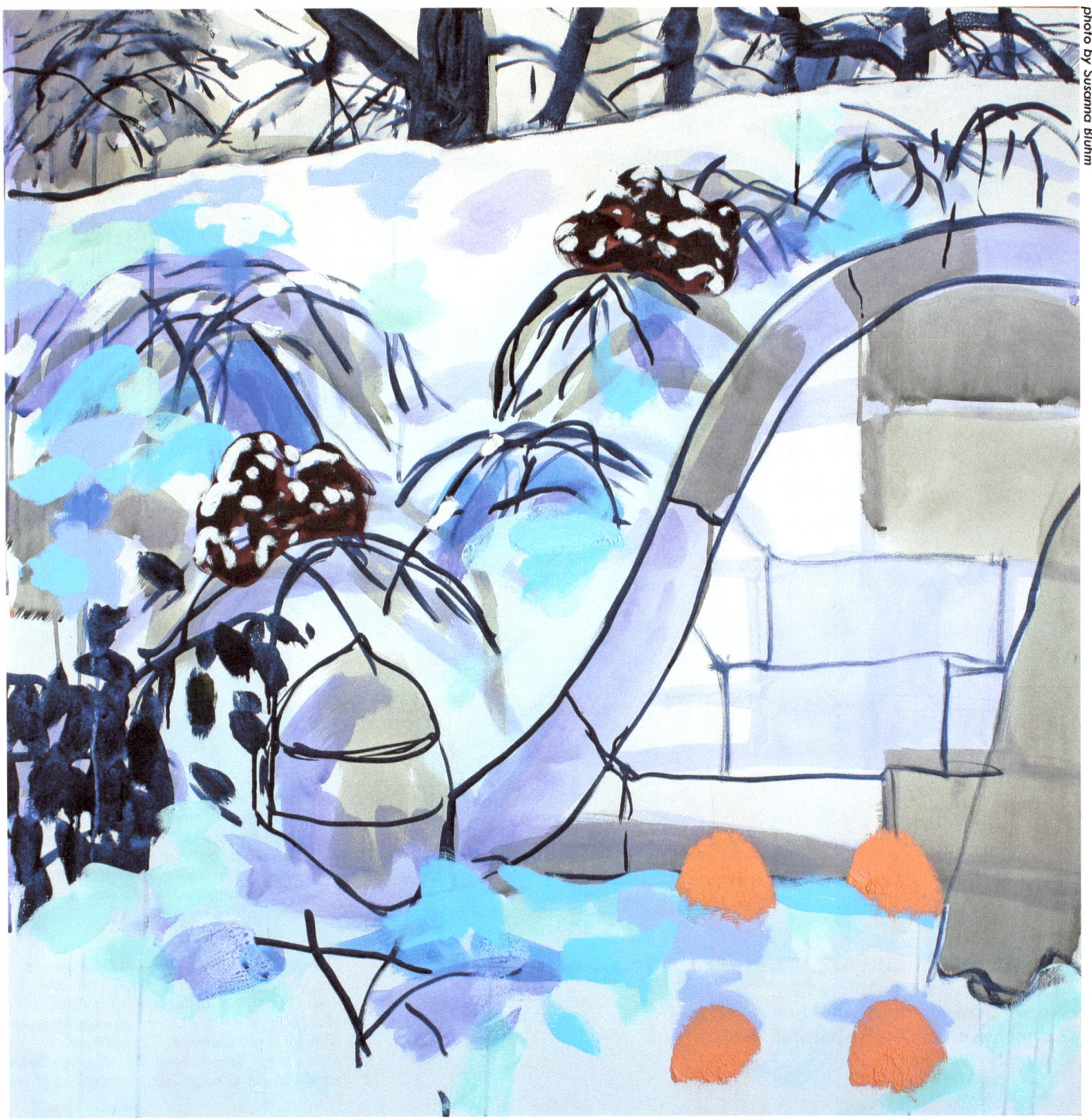

photo by Susanna Bluhm

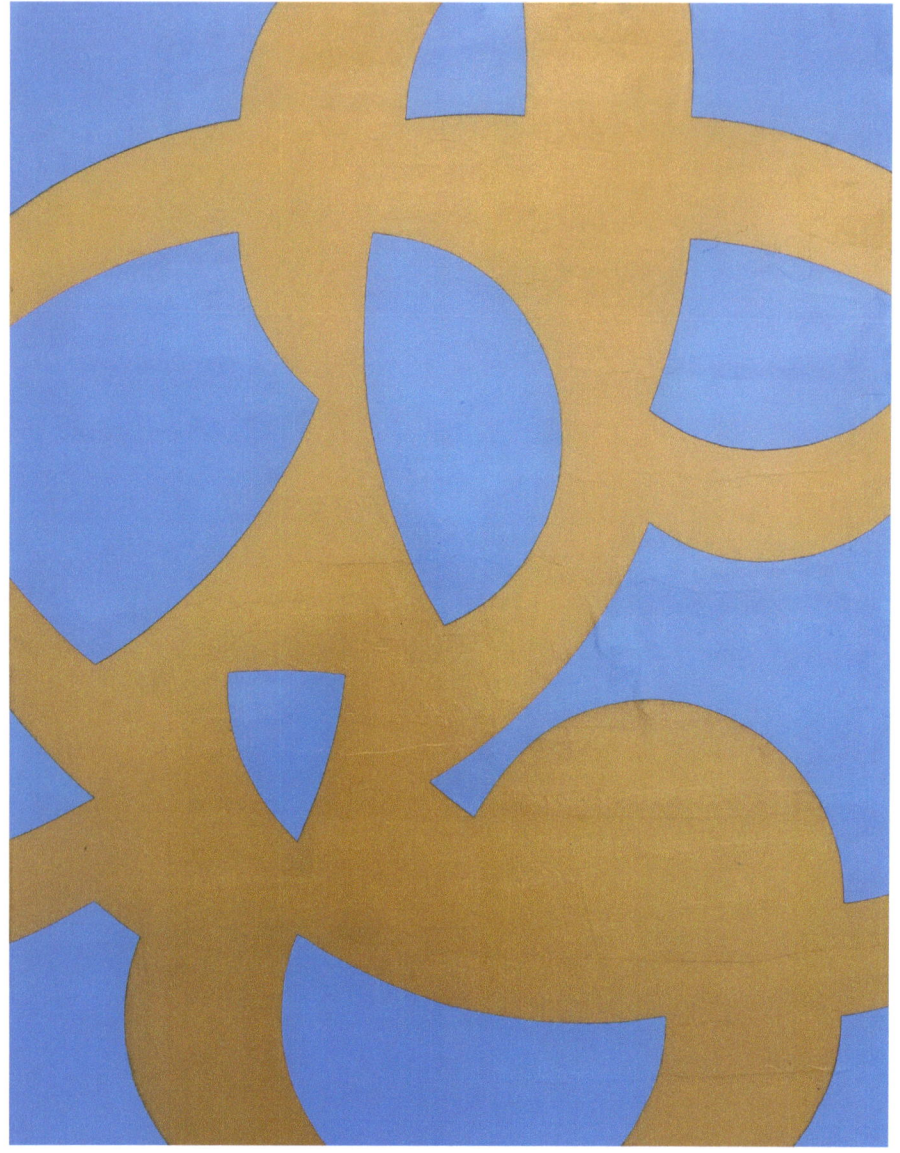

Jazz Brown

Jazz Brown is an autodidact who uses acrylic paint to create vivid, expressive compositions. His artistic approach presents intense vibration through contrasting hues, shapes, and textures. He is inspired by both the Minimalism art movement and the Bebop jazz offspring from the 1960s. Brown describes his technique as "consciousnesses on canvas."

sourcelessness
Acrylic, paper on panel, 20 x 16", 2018

"Exercising geometric, text and hard edged proficiency, I explore the contrast between the eternal nature of oneness and the false perception of duality."

Exercising geometric, text and hard edged proficiency, I explore the contrast between the eternal nature of oneness and the false perception of duality. Using the present moment as a point of reference, I reveal both formlessness as truth and form as a vehicle of consciousness to experience the wonder of the infinite.

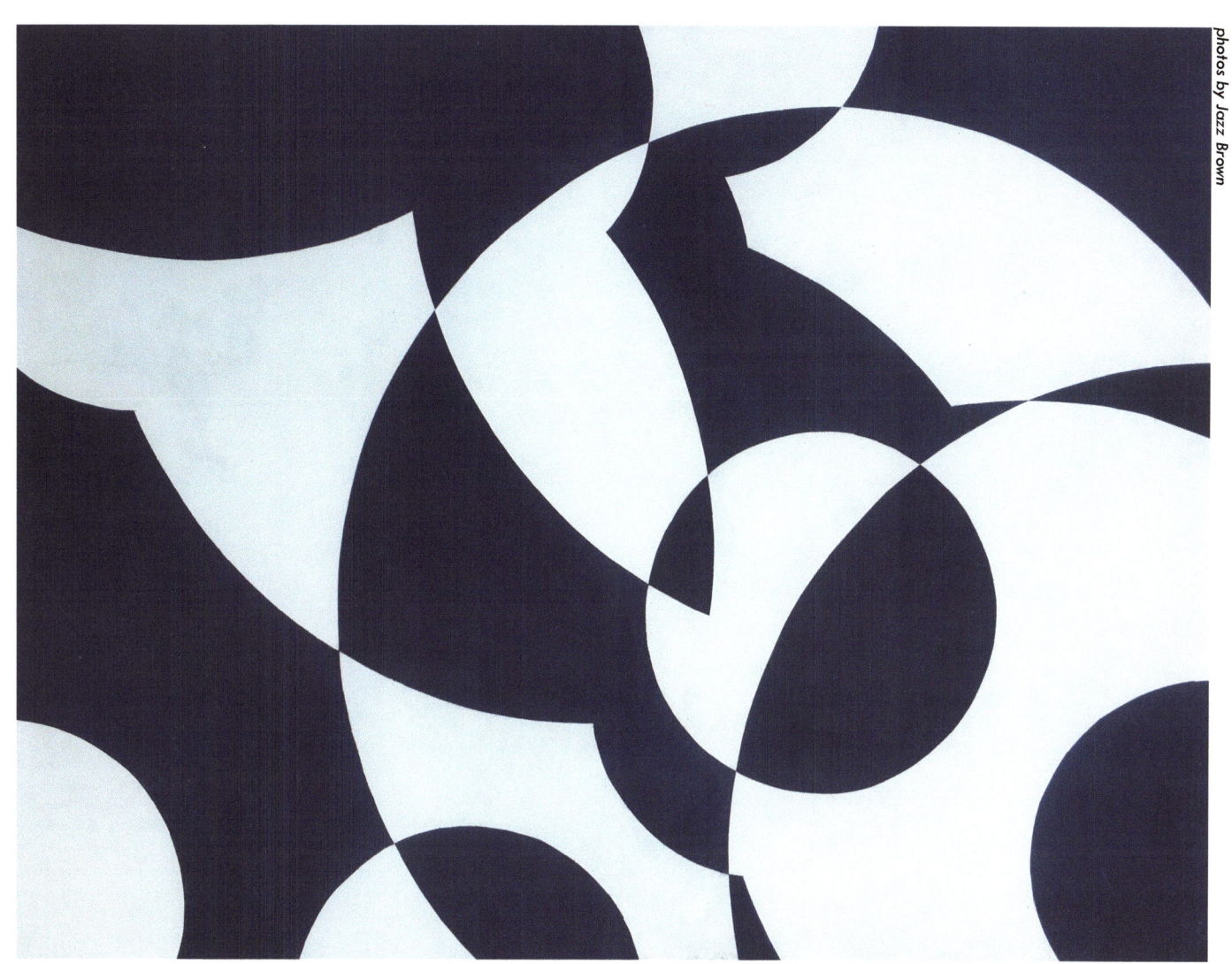

photos by Jazz Brown

the illusion of mind
Acrylic on panel, 18 x 24", 2018

Center on Contemporary Art   Jazz Brown

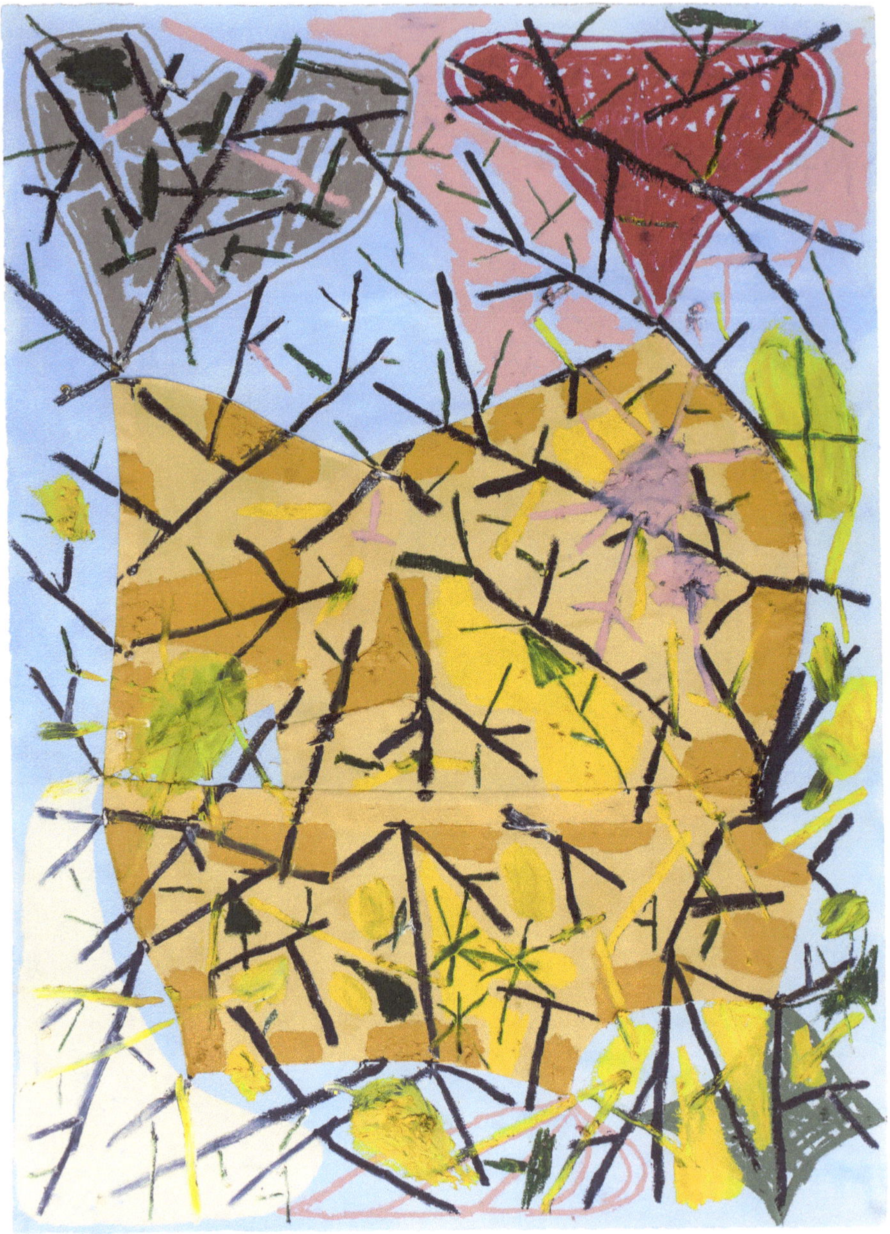

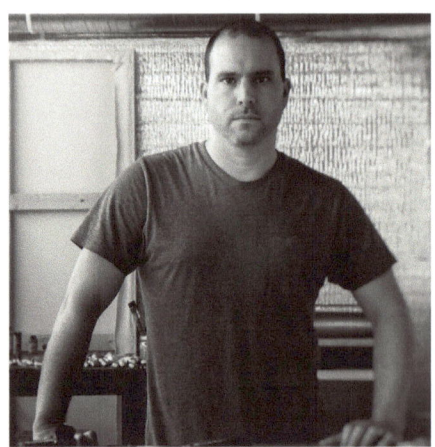

Brian Cypher

Brian Cypher (Yuma, AZ 1974) is a self taught artist living and working in Skagit Valley, Washington. Over the past twenty plus years, Cypher has been showing his artwork throughout the United States and Europe. Cypher works primarily with drawing, painting and printmaking. His marks represent an intersection between the observed and the unknown. He reveals a visual language through primitive gestures and symbols. The work is based in formal abstraction that culls from observation, nature, and invented iconography. He finds his imagery through the process of drawing and material investigation; an open ended approach to allow for a constant flow of ideas, tangents, and detours to occur. The spaces created in the work tend to generate familiar yet unknown associations.

Buried Under Branches and Blues
Acrylic, fabric and oil stick on paper, 51 x 38", 2017

Painters Who Fucking Know How to Paint   Center on Contemporary Art

photos by Brian Cypher

"I paint and assign meaning; the feedback loop of thinking. An image formed from impulse; the record of a built language."

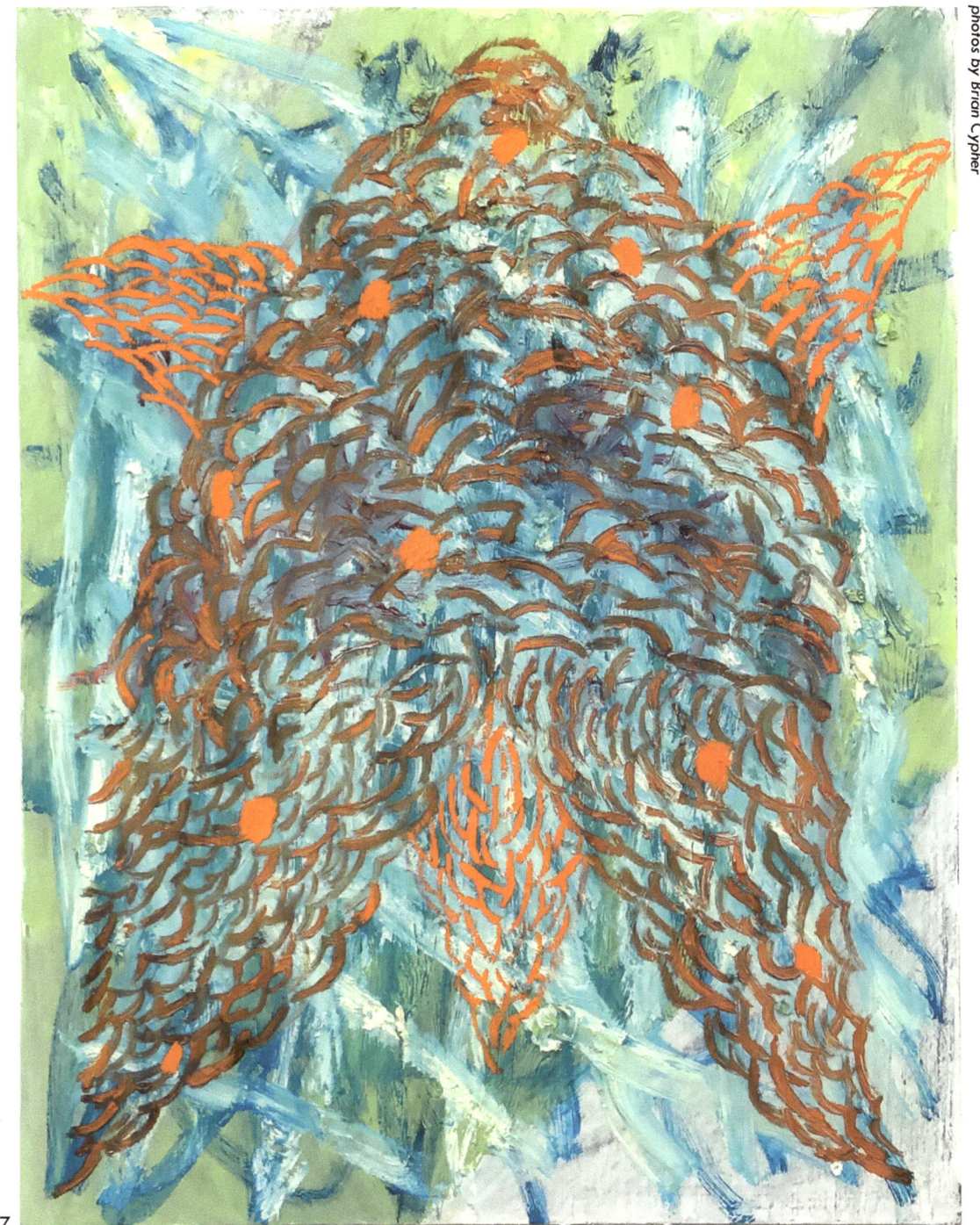

Fatal Flower
Oil on panel, 20 x 16", 2017

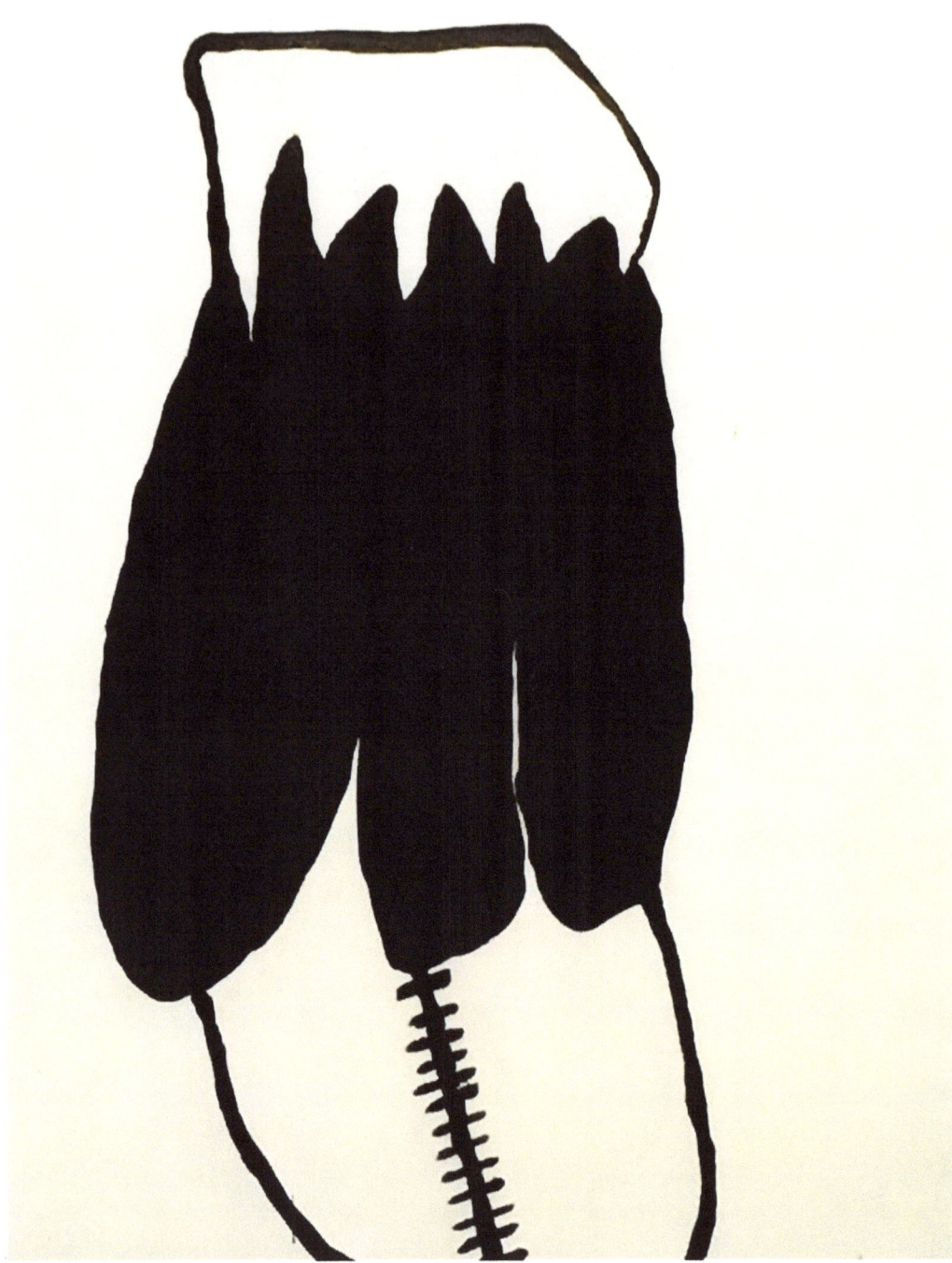

"As an artist I strive to transform and codify historical information into a visual abstract language... As I proceed, the language morphs into a unique melding of imagination and facts. Each piece produced is free of direct reference but underpinned by the original information."

You Tried
Vinyl paint on board
30 x 24", 2018

Carole d'Inverno

Center on Contemporary Art

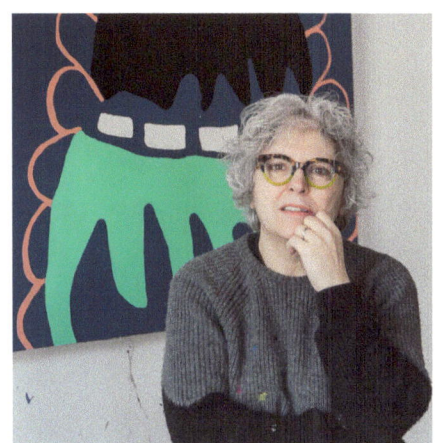

Carole d'Inverno

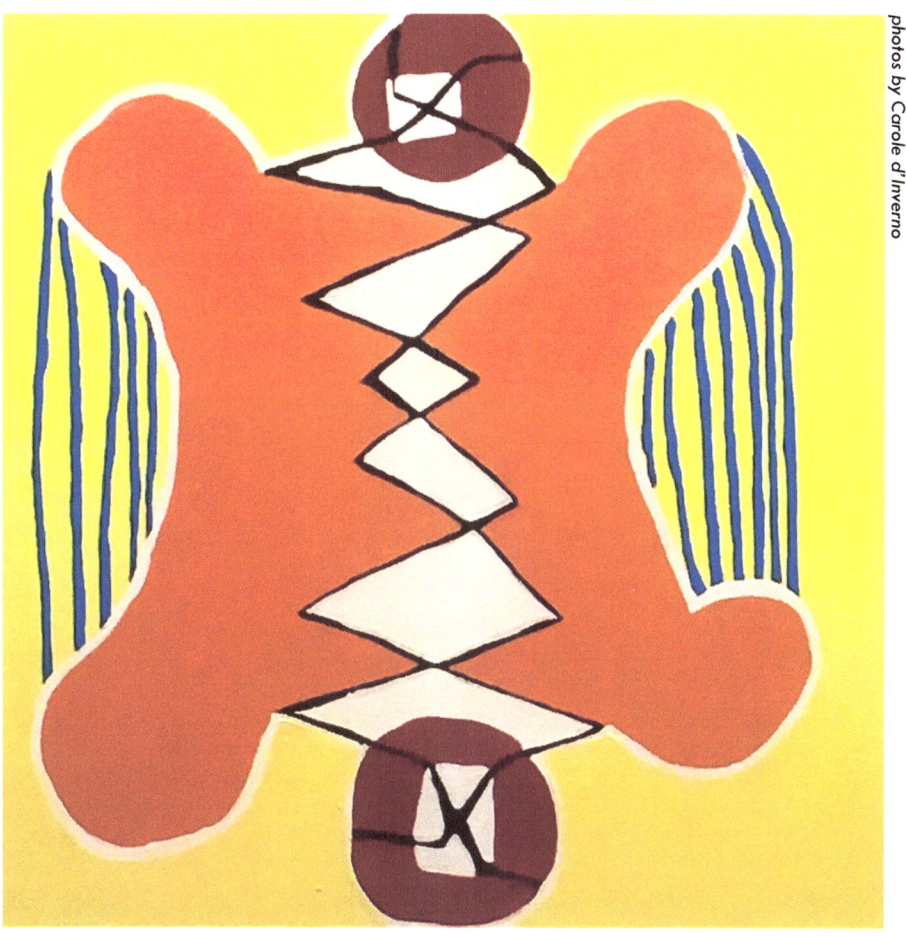

photos by Carole d'Inverno

Carole d'Inverno was born in 1956 and grew up in Italy and Belgium. She moved to the United States in 1979 and now lives in Brooklyn, New York.

d'Inverno has had numerous solo and group shows in the United States and is the recipient of many awards and honors including: Artist in Residence Art and History Museums, Maitland, Florida; Solo Show at the Massillon Museum of Art and History, Massillon, Ohio; National Competition Winner "The Art of Ivy Side" solo show at PENN State Altoona, PA; solo show at the Western Carolina University Art Center; solo show at SUNY Rochester Monroe College, Rochester, NY; fellowships and residencies at La Playa (Summer Lake, OR), Willapa Bay Air, (Willapa, WA), the Vermont Studio Center, (Johnson, VT), the BAU Institute (Otranto, Italy), Starry Night (Truth or Consequences, NM), and the Wassard Elia Center (Ascea, Italy).
Her work is in the public collections of the Microsoft Art Collection, Kirkland, WA; Group Health Headquarters, Seattle; Swedish Hospital, Seattle; Seattle University, Seattle; and in private collections across the US and Europe.

Carole d'Inverno is married to musician/composer Bill Frisell and they have a daughter, photographer and videographer Monica Jane Frisell.

There Were Rumors
Vinyl paint on board, 30 x 30", 2018

A deep interest in American History is at the core of all my work. As an artist I strive to transform and codify historical information into a visual abstract language. To prepare for a new series, I extensively research a place, a time period, an event. From the information gathered, I then develop a visual coded language with repetitive motives, patterns and colors specific to the subject I am working on.

As I proceed, the language morphs into a unique melding of imagination and facts. Each piece produced is free of direct reference but underpinned by the original information. History is of course made of Science, Politics, Art, etc., and this richness allows me to investigate and explore far and wide. As a result each series is unique and as much about the details as the sweeping historical facts.

"I'm moved by color and the way light plays with objects as well as scenes that we tend to take for granted or are so mundane they become invisible."

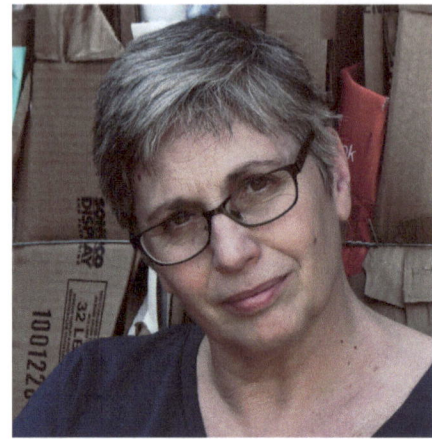

Marie Gagnon

Born to a painter and a physician, Marie's mother was her first painting teacher. There were many stops and starts in Marie's journey to paint as she struggled with the practicality of pursuing such a life, but the pull of passion was strong and at 36 years old, completed her BFA in painting. After 13 years in Seattle, she returned to New England in April 2012 and relocated in Providence RI. In Seattle, Marie had the privilege of enjoying a studio space for 4 years in the historic and beloved 619 Western Arts building before the artists were evicted in September 2011 due to the pending viaduct demolition and structural building issues. Her studio is now located on the west side of Providence.

As a painter, culture warrior and an avid observer, I paint what captures my heart and eye. I'm moved by color and the way light plays with objects as well as scenes that we tend to take for granted or are so mundane they become invisible. I enjoy reworking the same view in different ways, ever curious as to how it can be transformed.

When I'm not emotionally engaged with a specific subject matter, I always return to still life. The most accessible objects are the ones on my painting table. A few months back, I was carelessly holding my camera while it was on, happened to look at the screen and became excited. The camera showed me a new viewpoint.

As I was working these new paintings, I was consumed with concept, agonizing over what the work was trying to say. It became toxic to my painting. If I stumble upon a deeper concept, it happens organically, evolving with the work.

One day in the studio I just screamed out loud to myself "screw the concept, just fucking paint!" I laughed and in that, accessed the freedom to continue... to paint just because.

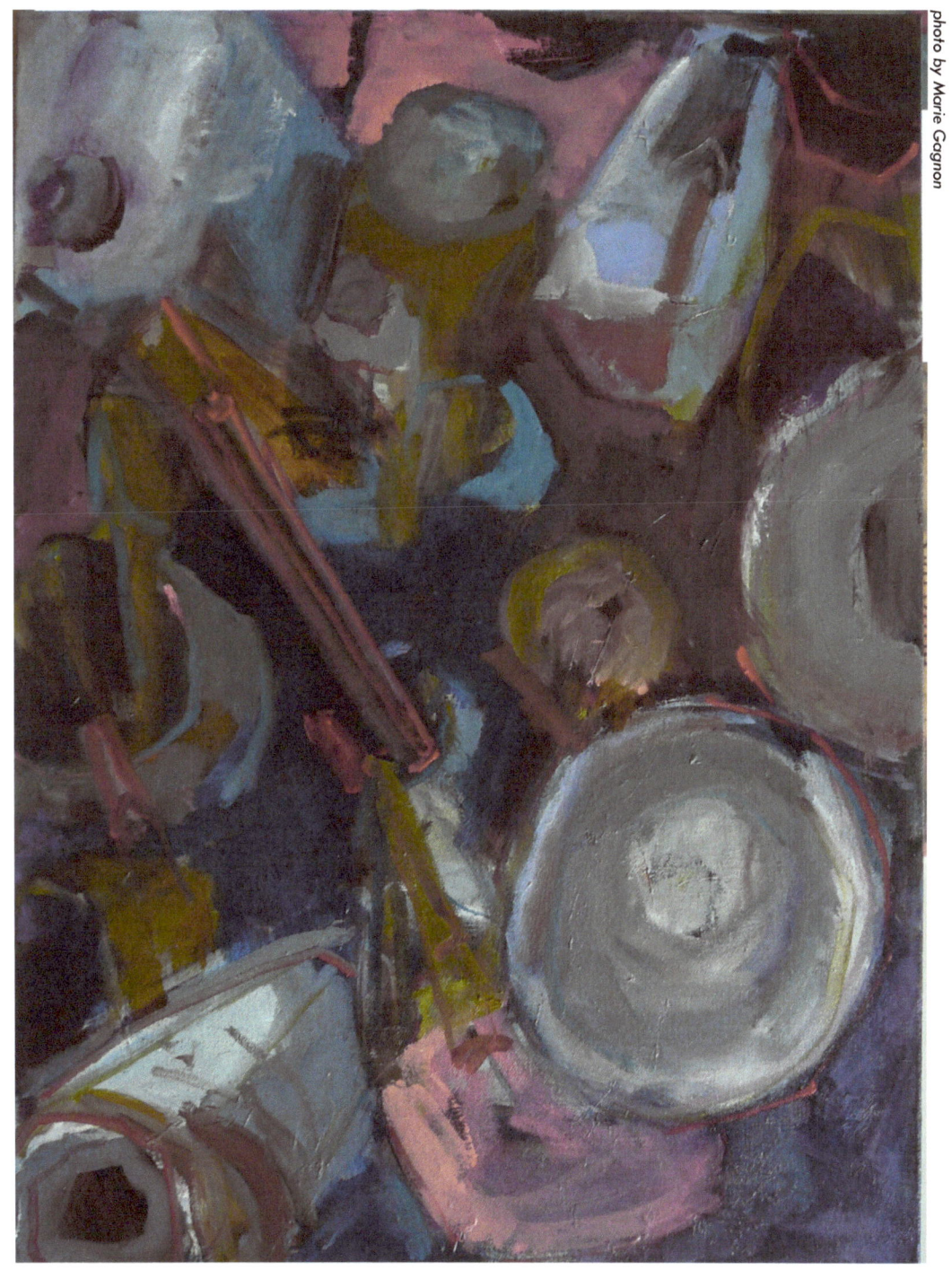

photo by Marie Gagnon

Untitled 1
From the "Screw The Concept" series
Oil on canvas, 24 x 18", 2018

Center on Contemporary Art   Marie Gagnon

"My studies of geometry, space, light and color in my woods is in search of elusive emotional qualities our forests offer us."

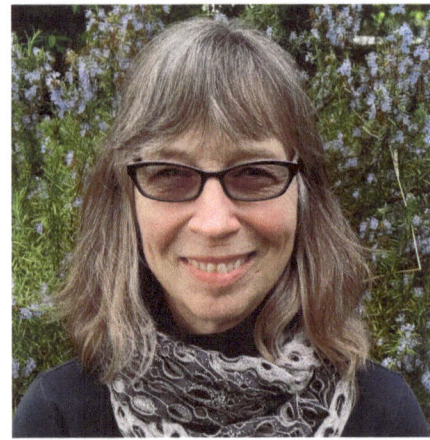

Kathy Gore Fuss

Kathy Gore Fuss was born in Seattle (1955), but spent most of her childhood in the Mid-West (Kansas and Indiana). Her family returned to the Pacific Northwest in 1966 where she went on to complete high school, and graduate from the University of Washington with a BFA in Drawing and Painting. She has made Olympia, Washington her home since 1980. In 2004, her husband of 23 years died suddenly of a heart attack. The ten years following his death involved an arduous process of rebuilding which included, designing and building a new studio (2010), shifting her practice to plein air painting (2011) and organizing, fundraising and introducing her painting workshops (2012). She is represented by the Prographica Gallery, Seattle, Washington and has been awarded an Artist Residency for August 2018 at Jentel, Wyoming.

The Pacific Northwest forests have been my source material for my paintings and drawings for over a decade. The choice to move my painting practice outdoors was precipitated by the tranquility I felt from utilizing what I had at hand to reclaim and regenerate my soul: our woods. Standing and painting on site for hours over the course of weeks and months opened up new opportunities to renew my relationship with nature and has allowed my painting and drawing to flourish.

I have also witnessed numerous conflicts over my lifetime regarding the wealth of our state's resources and the demands our northwest population places on them. Economics, land management and livelihoods are all vying for projections and outcomes that can be identified as "sustainable".

"... Trees call us to a state of mindfulness where we become better in tune with and more compassionate toward our surroundings. Trees are complex, beautiful, fragile and strong. Because of these characteristics, I think of them as ambassadors for the rest of nature." -- Nalini M. Nadkarni, Between Earth and Sky

"Acts of creation are ordinarily reserved for gods and poets, but humbler folk may circumvent this restriction if they know how. To plant a pine, for example, one need be neither god nor poet; one need only own a shovel." ? Aldo Leopold

My studies of geometry, space, light and color in my woods is in search of elusive emotional qualities our forests offer us. I hope to pay homage in some small way to the ecosystems that are working every day, rain or shine, providing us the high quality of life we call "living in the Pacific Northwest".

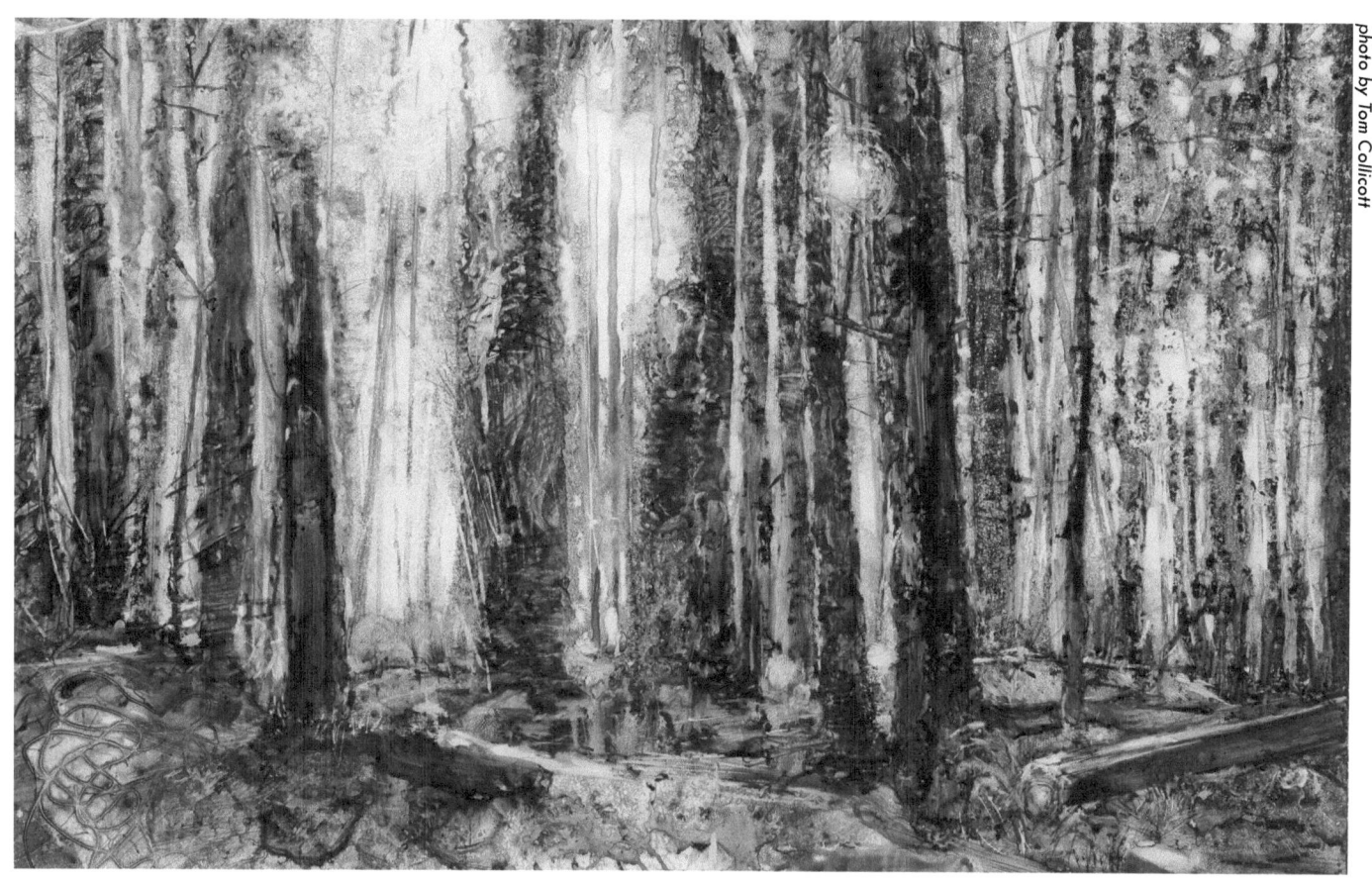

photo by Tom Collicott

Timber
Walnut ink on YUPO, 13.25 x 21", 2017

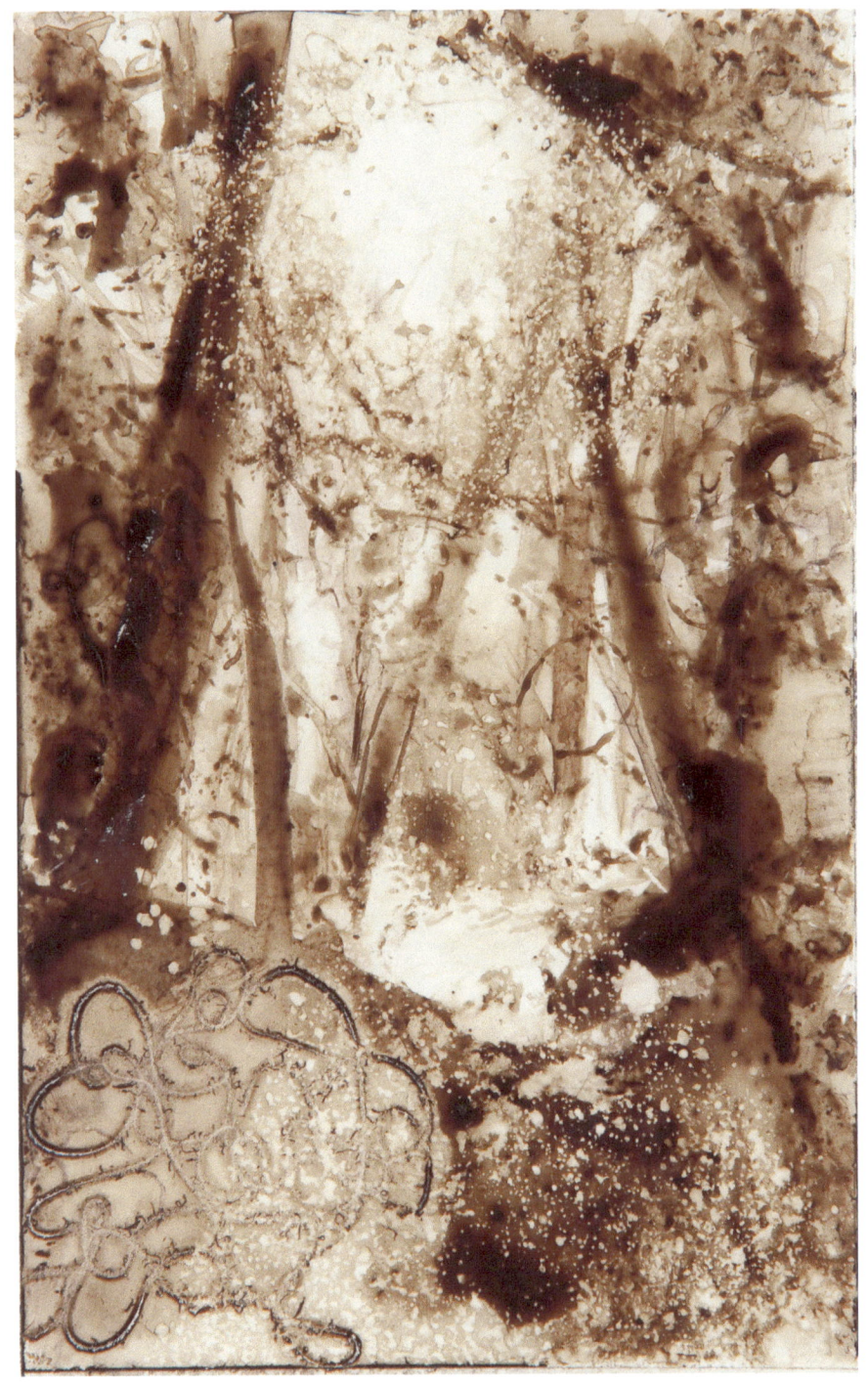

I Call This Home
Walnut ink on YUPO, 5.5 x 3.5", 2017

Painters Who Fucking Know How to Paint

Center on Contemporary Art

photos by Tom Collicott

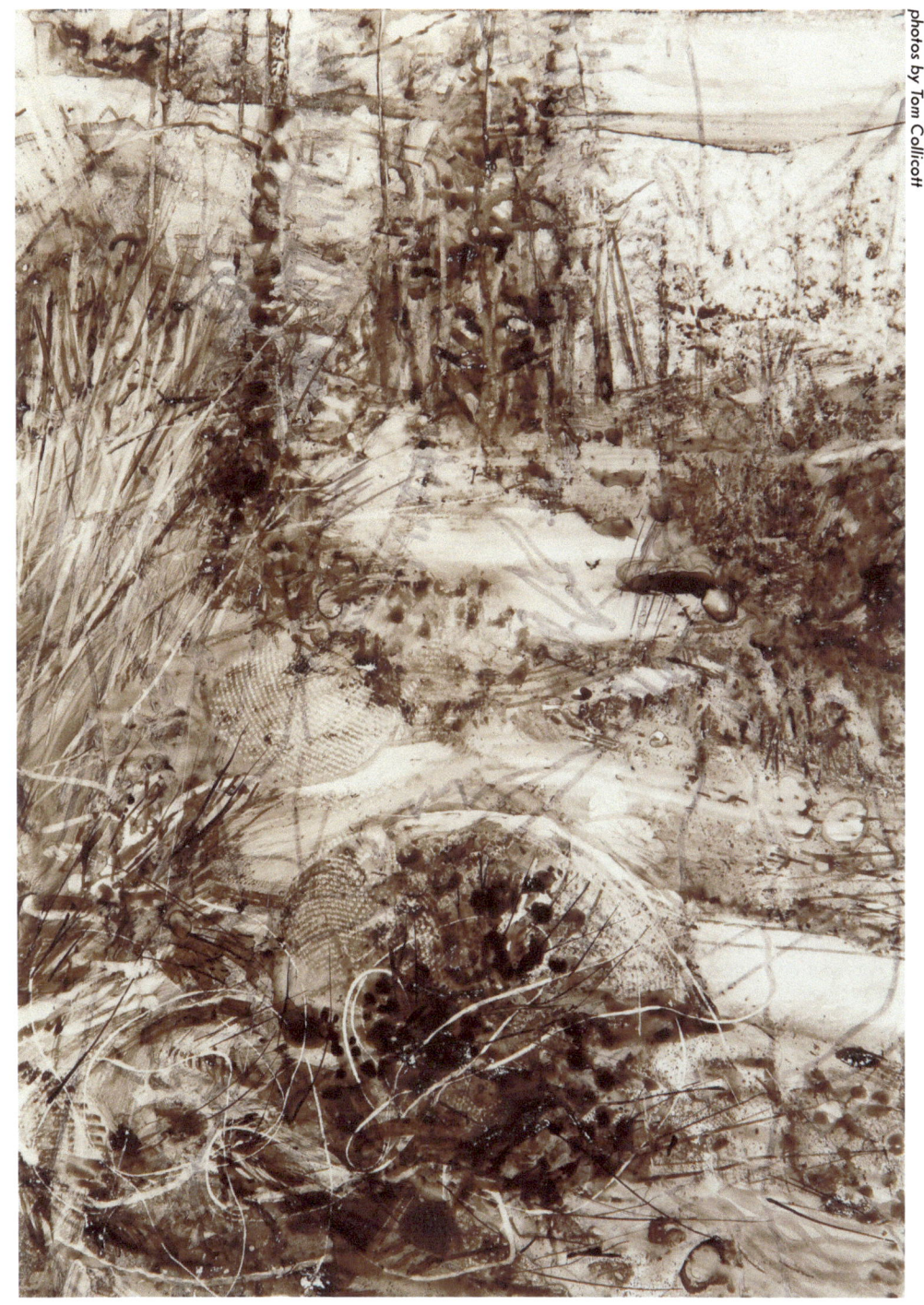

Undisturbed
Walnut ink on YUPO
7.25 x 5.25", 2017

Center on Contemporary Art

Kathy Gore Fuss

Cable Griffith

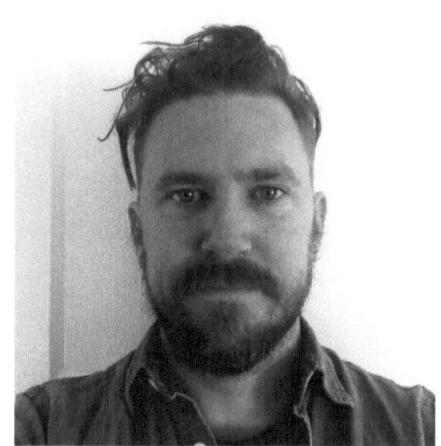

Cable Griffith is an artist, curator, and educator living and working in Seattle, WA. Griffith has exhibited nationally and internationally, including G. Gibson Gallery, the Frye Art Museum, Bellevue Arts Museum, the Whatcom Museum, and Aqua Art Fair (Miami), and the NEoN Digital Arts Festival in Dundee, Scotland. He has received numerous awards and commissions, including a large installation at Seattle-Tacoma International Airport. Griffith's work is in multiple collections, including Microsoft, Vulcan, Weyerhaeuser, Capitol One, and the Washington State Art Collection. Curatorially, he served as Kirkland Arts Center's Exhibitions Director from 2007-2010 and as Exhibitions Curator at Cornish College of the Arts from 2010-2014. Griffith received a BFA from Boston University and an MFA from the University of Washington. He is a professor at Cornish College of the Arts and is represented in Seattle by G. Gibson Gallery.

Influenced by modernist painting and early video game imagery, my recent work explores the connections and potentials of both. Notions of play, practice, improvisation, and exploration add an additional narrative to the relationship of symbols, actions, and reactions.

"To me, the process of painting in an appropriate metaphor for life. A series of decisions, layered over time, correcting missteps through addition, towards a state of balance. One mark leads to another, then another, as one painting leads to another, and yet another. Meaning can only come from the opportunity to step back and observe from some distance, understanding the moment in relationship to the past."

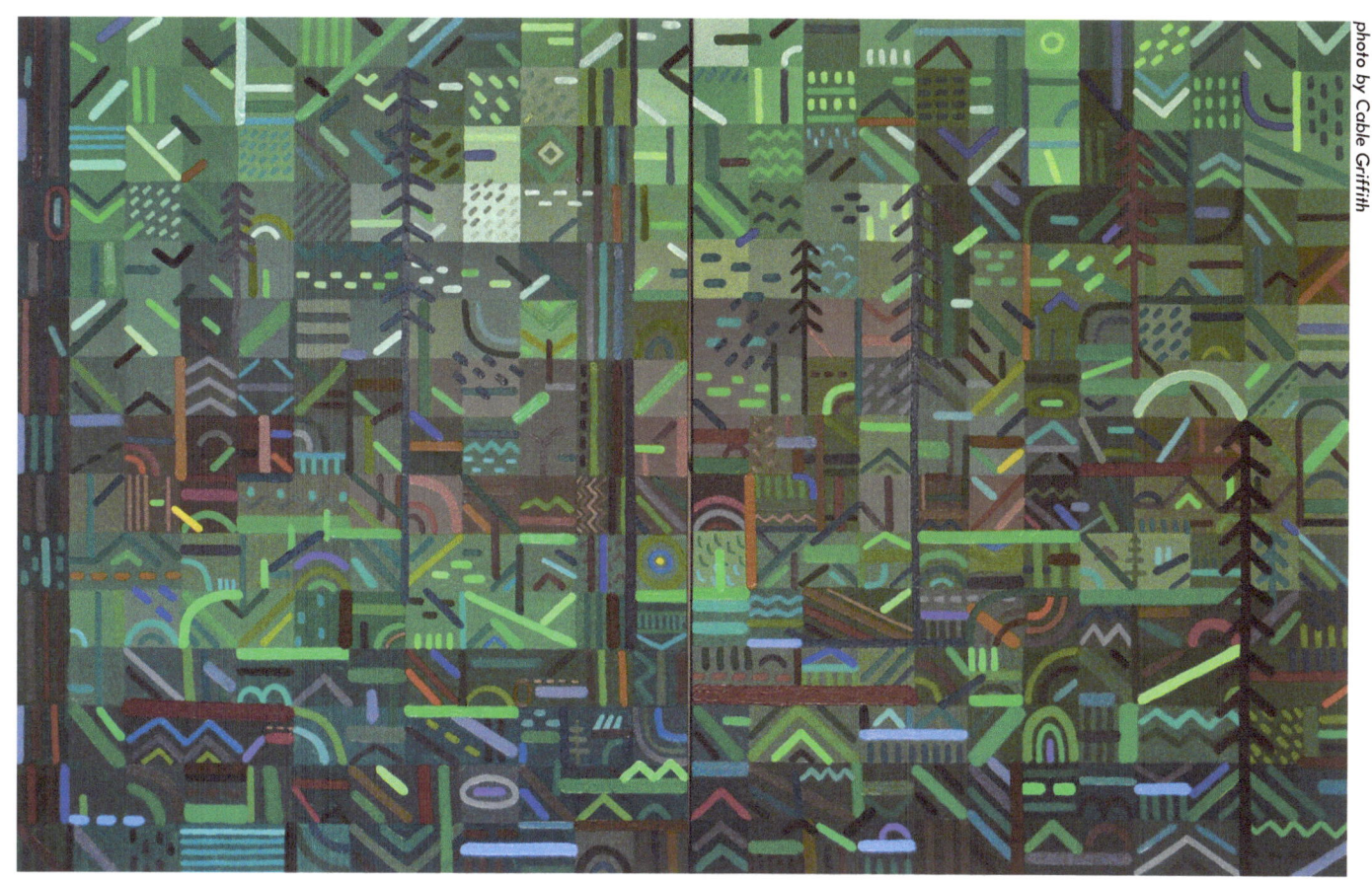

Halle Ravine, NY
Acrylic and oil on canvas, 30 x 48", 2016

photo by Cable Griffith

"I am interested in manipulating pictorial space to create a sense of imbalance, a space that is not quite what one would find in the world."

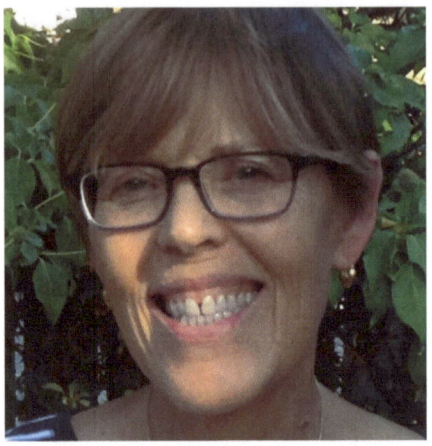

Patricia Hagen

Patricia Hagen is a Pacific Northwest native, born in Portland Oregon, who has lived, worked, traveled studied and shown throughout the United States. She received her B.F.A. from Miami University in Oxford, Ohio and her M.F.A. from California College of the Arts in Oakland, California.

In addition to having shown in galleries in Seattle, New York, San Francisco, San Diego, and other states she has been a selected artist featured in the national publication "New American Painting" in 1996, 2005,2007 and 2016. Her work is included in the collections of the King County Arts Commission; the Nordstrom Corporation, and others.

Picture Maker

I am a painter. I paint to play, to surprise myself, and to uncover something new from deep inside.

My earliest influences were graphic cartoons such as Rocky and Bullwinkle, and I hope that shows. Both my forms and the quality of my lines are directly connected to these cartoons. It is important to me that my forms have a certain casualness of character to them, an awkward gesture. I make what I call big dumb shapes. This is hard to explain, but it is this awkwardness that makes the work feel very human – a big lumbering oaf, sincerely trying to do what is right and just missing the mark.

I live in the Pacific Northwest, and see mountains, water, clouds, and gray skies.These are the things that I paint, this is my current palette. Monumental forms can invoke a certain awe in humans, like the grand emotion of standing before large bodies of water. In my new work, the environment itself has become a big rough-hewn character.

But I am not a painter of views. I am interested in manipulating pictorial space to create a sense of imbalance, a space that is not quite what one would find in the world. This imbalance is crucial to me because it causes the brain to flip from seeing pictorial depth to seeing two-dimensional paint on canvas.

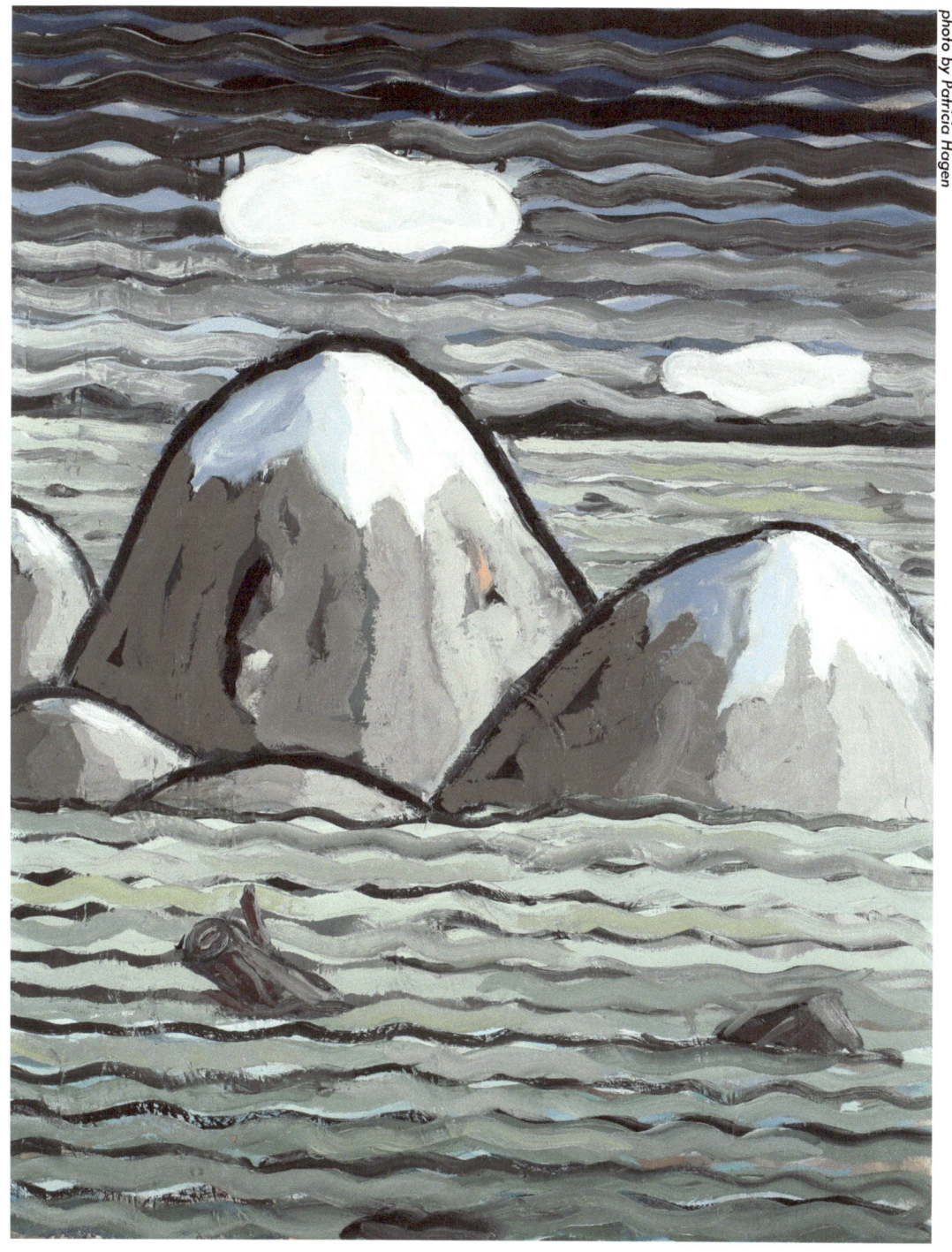

photo by Patricia Hagen

Debris
Oil on canvas, 28 x 22", 2017

Center on Contemporary Art

Patricia Hagen

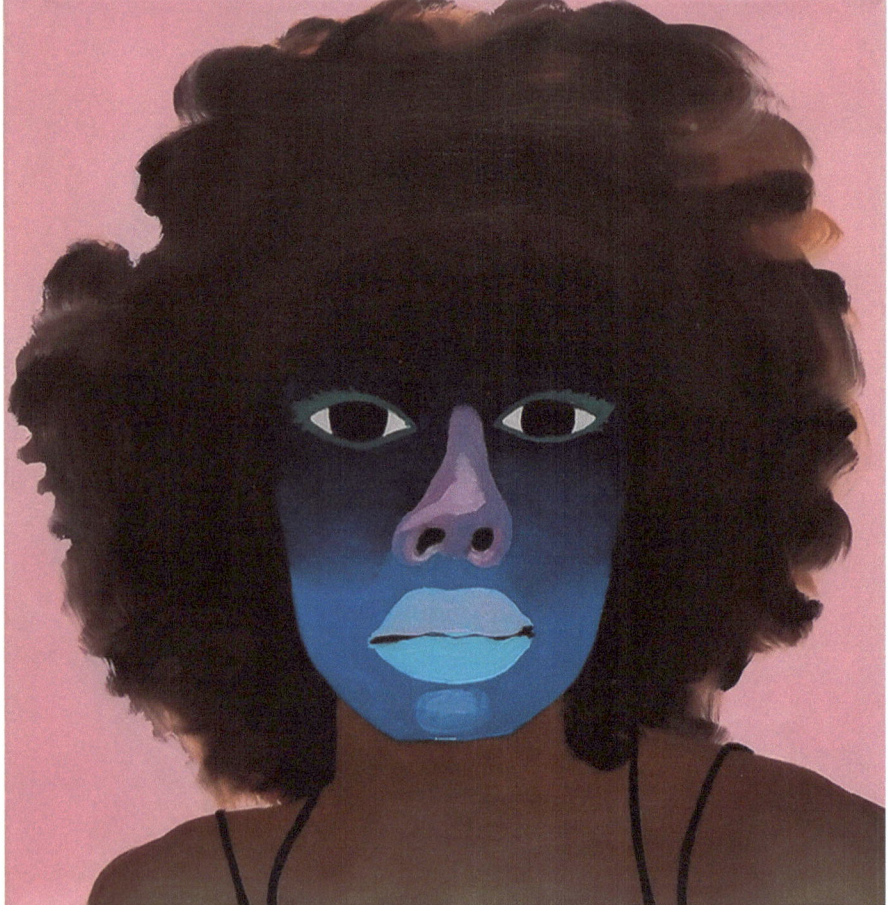

Selfie Portrait Series #4
Oil on canvas, 14 x 14", 2018

"I want the viewers of my work to not only become directly engaged with the imagery, but to also walk away feeling as if they've learned something."

Ronald Hall's paintings are a kaleidoscopic fusion of urban energy, figurative and narrative by nature. Growing up amidst the crime ridden neighborhoods of Pittsburgh, led him to see art as both an informative and educational teaching tool. Born out of stories of fictional and or non-fictional perspectives of an African American artist, his paintings attempt to challenge the viewers interpretation of what contemporary black art is. Ronald's work has been exhibited in numerous galleries and art museums internationally and throughout the US. A 2016 Skowhegan School of Painting and Sculpture alumnus, Ronald also studied Illustration at the Art Institute of Pittsburgh. Ronald is currently working on a new body of work that will include Video and painting, and will continue to explore issues and themes that are affecting African Americans and popular culture within historical and contemporary contexts.

Ronald Hall

My work is intended to create thought-provoking and narrative interpretations of historical and contemporary African American themes and related issues. Often loosely based on fictional and or non-fictional stories, these narrative images also strive to provoke the human emotion, to ask questions, to spark a dialogue pertaining to race relations involving human interactions and reactions of and towards the subject matter in various ways. For most of the paintings that I make, the computer plays an important role in the development process as far as color experimentation, compositional arrangements of elements, and scale. The images used for the collages in some of the paintings can come from various sources such as African American history books, newspapers, or internet resources. I want the viewers of my work to not only become directly engaged with the imagery, but to also walk away feeling as if they've learned something about themselves or about the relevancy of dealing with social or political issues in contemporary art from the perspective of an African American artist.

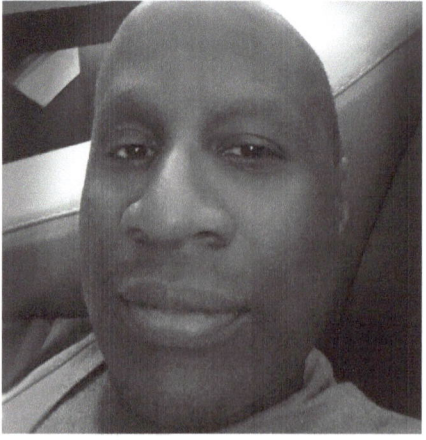

Painters Who Fucking Know How to Paint   Center on Contemporary Art

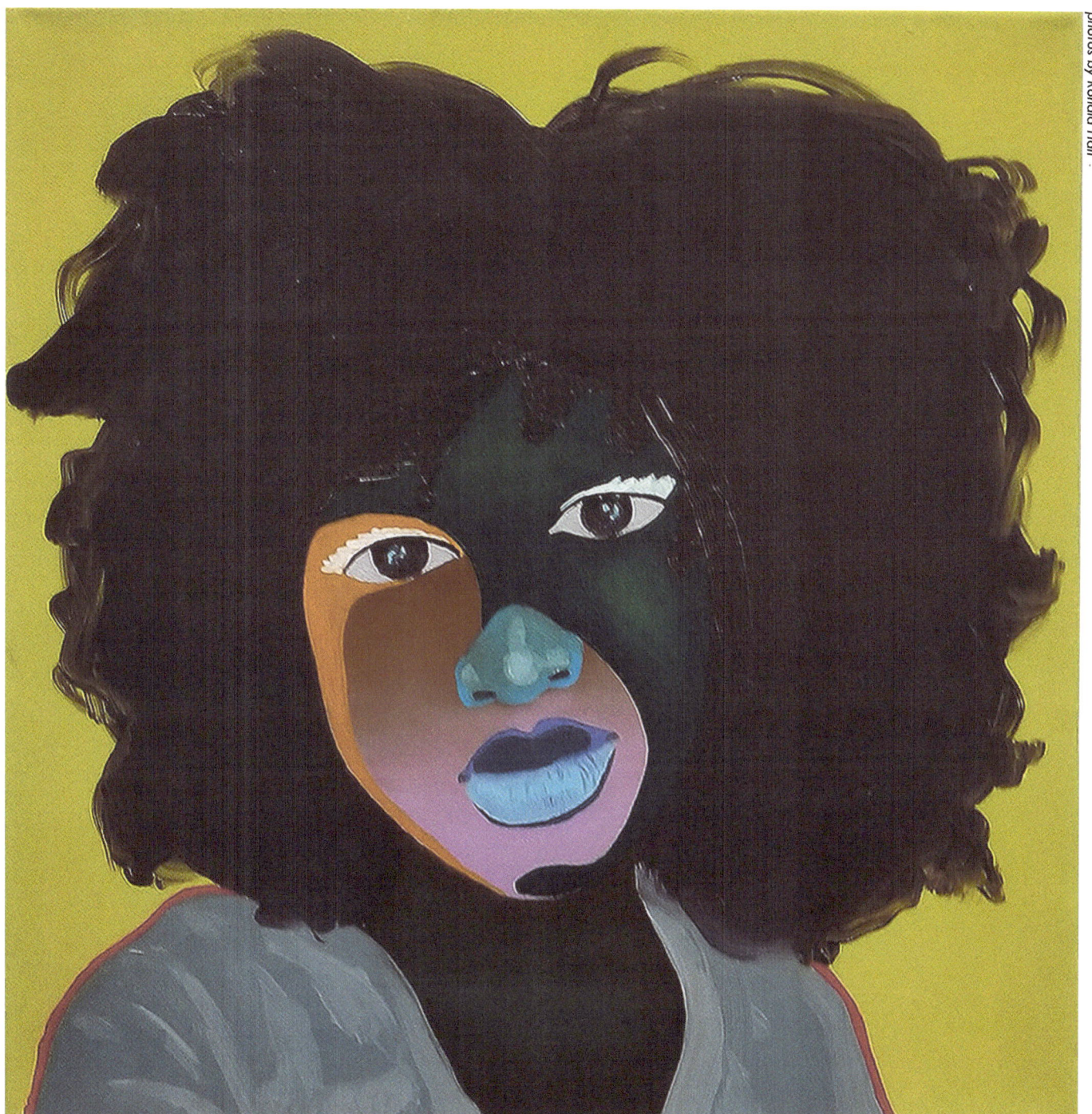

"When I am painting, my goal is to be overtaken by a force larger than myself — to succumb to the whims of the spiraling internal debates, that I cannot hope to unwind with words."

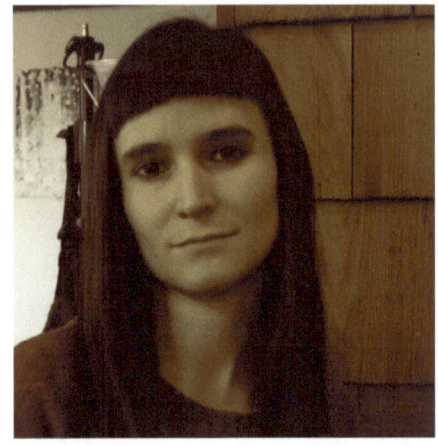

Laura Hamje

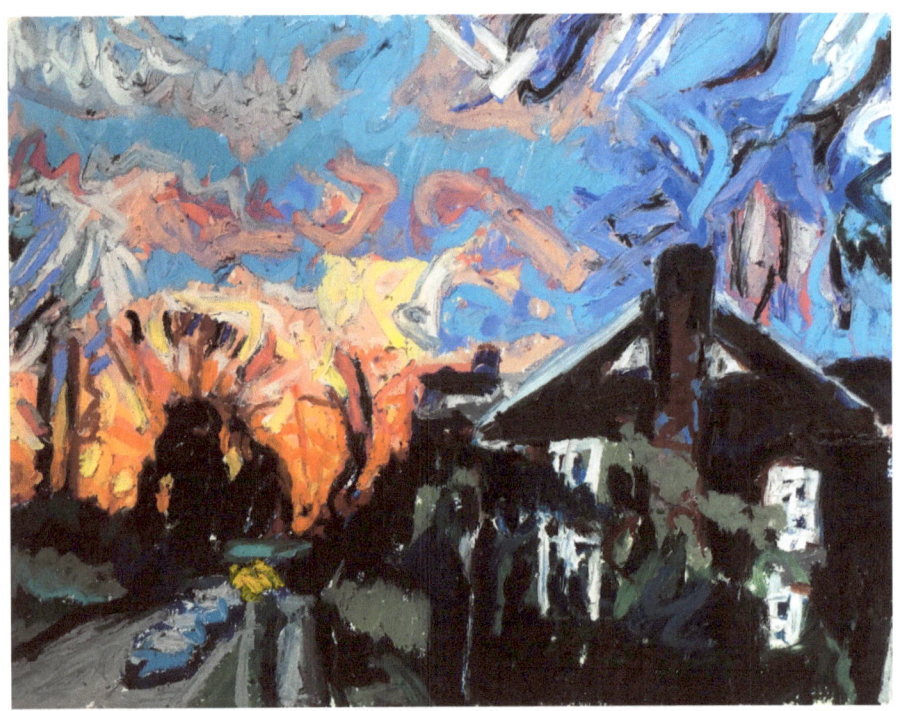

Laura Hamje is an oil painter from Austin, Texas, working in Seattle since 2004, and is represented by Bryan Ohno Gallery. Laura received her BFA from the University of Washington in 2008 and has worked as a staff accountant for 12 years. Laura co-founded/operated Blindfold Gallery (2012-2014), which specialized in showing work by emerging artists and hosted free poetry/music/art events. Laura has shown her work in Seattle, Astoria, OR, Los Angeles and NYC. Her work is included in the corporate collections of Perkins Coie and Weyerhaeuser.

Mirage
Oil pastel on paper, 15 x 18" framed, 2017

I feel a growing separation between nature and the developed world. I internalize the conflict; it lives within me as an ongoing battle, swelling and receding, like waves. When I am painting, my goal is to be overtaken by a force larger than myself — to succumb to the whims of the spiraling internal debates, that I cannot hope to unwind with words.

Painters Who Fucking Know How to Paint   Center on Contemporary Art

photos by Laura Hamje

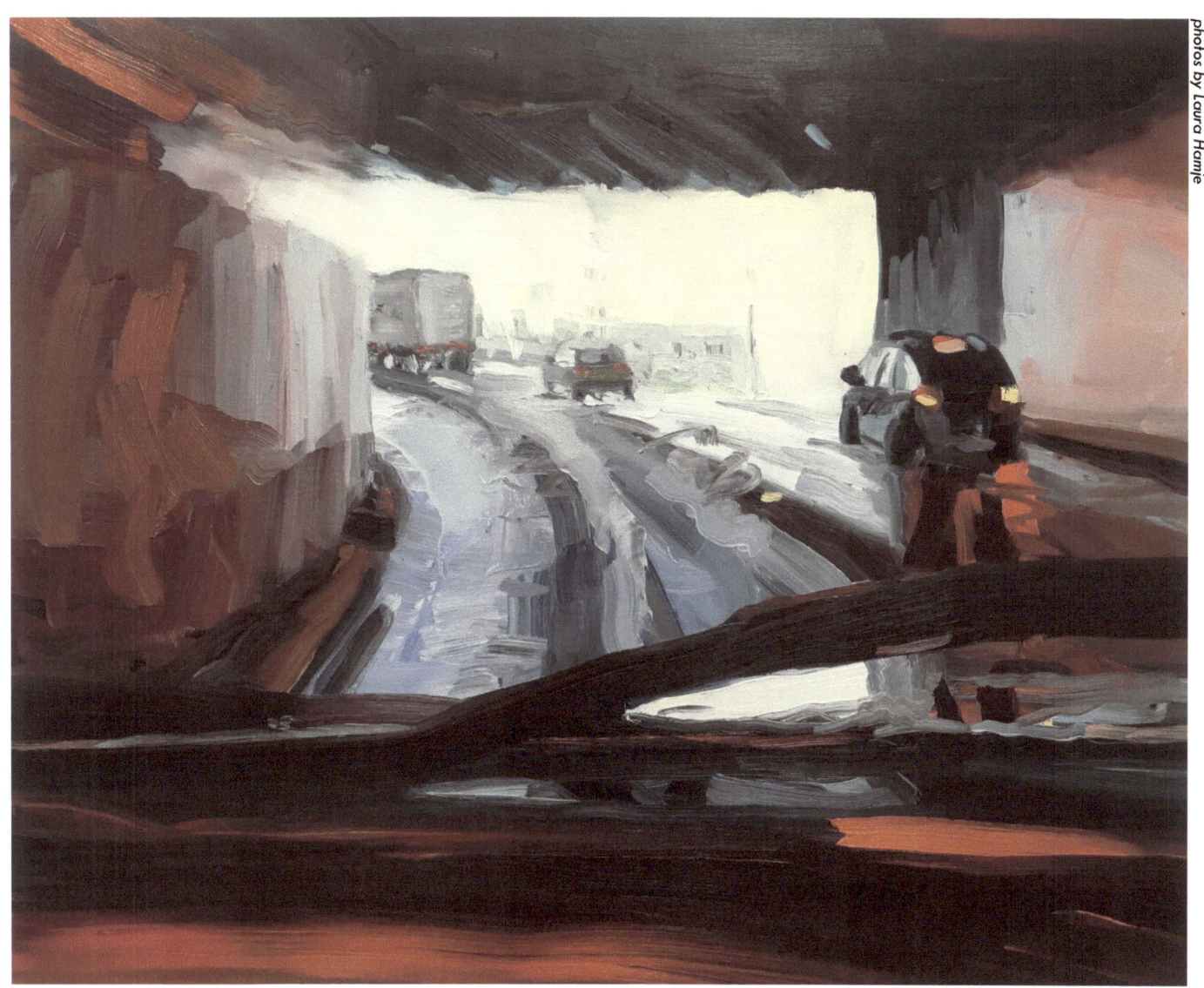

Seeing Red
Oil on board, 12 x 16", 2018

"I want materials to guide the work toward what it is going to be, while maintaining a consistent language across media. I believe that by allowing only a few variables to exist the materials are forced to reveal their nuances. This permits my personal vocabulary to speak louder."

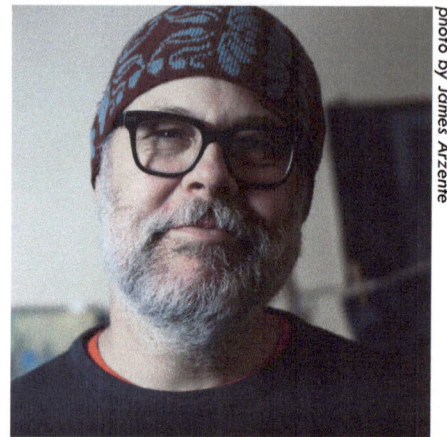

photo by James Arzente

Robert Hardgrave

Born in Oxnard, California, Robert Hardgrave has made a significant contribution to visual arts in the Pacific Northwest for over a decade. A finalist for the 2014 and 2016 Cornish College of the Arts Neddy Award in Painting and nominee for the 2014 Portland Art Museum's Contemporary Northwest Arts Awards. Hardgrave has exhibited in numerous solo and group shows in Seattle, Los Angeles, San Francisco, Denver, Chicago, New York, and Madrid, Spain. Locally, Robert is a member of the Duwamish River Residency, and his work is part of the permanent collections of Microsoft, Starbucks, King County and the Achenbach Foundation for Graphic Arts. Robert will be exhibiting at Studio e in Seattle, WA, 2019.

I am constantly in search of those ideas that can be pushed in multiple directions and still push back. I want to be challenged in such a way where the evolution of ideas flow, keeping me excited to stay in the studio day after day.

I change media regularly and process each to a point where I feel proficient. This helps ideas feel fresh and uncharted. Each new material requires unique allowances; I want materials to guide the work toward what it is going to be, while maintaining a consistent language across media. I believe that by allowing only a few variables to exist the materials are forced to reveal their nuances. This permits my personal vocabulary to speak louder, conducing cross-pollination between media, where ideas, discovery and surprise reign supreme.

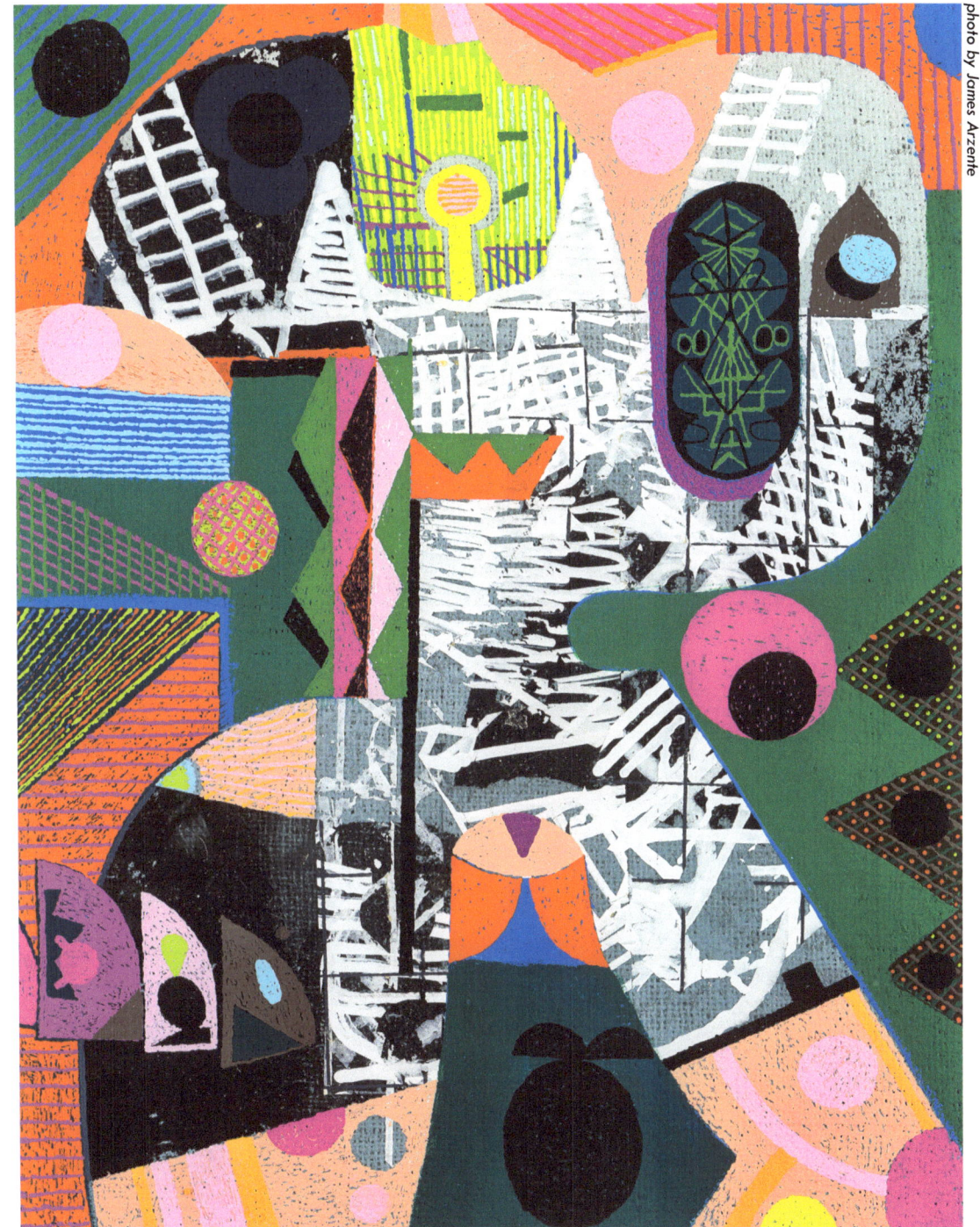

photo by James Arzente

black apple
Gouache on burlap
20 x 16", 2017

"When I enter the studio, I do not so much begin with an idea as endeavor to arrive at one... the examination of transference, information loss and facade [is] implicit in the work through the very techniques employed in its creation."

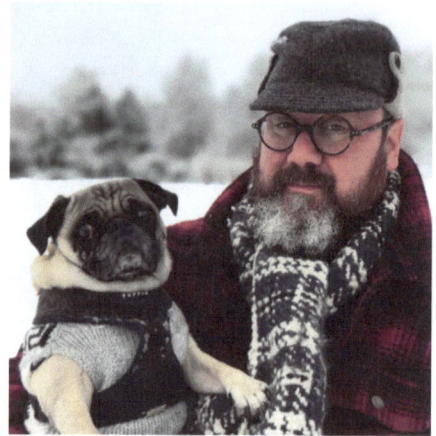

David Hytone

David Hytone was born in Des Moines, Iowa and left as soon as was practical. He currently lives and works in Seattle, Washington and is represented locally by Linda Hodges Gallery.

I've always said that when I enter the studio, I do not so much begin with an idea as endeavor to arrive at one.

In 2015 I began to create a new body of work that led to an examination of human frailty, and the mechanisms we employ to cope and compensate for our failings, imagined and otherwise. Soon the metric had begun to broaden, considering how these contrivances were performed on a societal level, how it is the nature of people, as individuals and societies, to constantly build and rebuild monuments to our existence, like carapaces around us, out of the ill-fitting remnants of our past coupled with the newfound symbols of our uncertain futures.

Soon I found parallels between these ideas of projection, facade and the mutability of identity with concepts found in the Holographic Model of theoretical physics. It seemed to me that the dodgy way reality presents itself to us was irrevocably tied to the way we present ourselves to the world, and conversely, ourselves. Information is always incomplete at best, and distorted by the very nature of our observation.

As was inferred above, my work is not necessarily about these ideas as much as these are questions that present themselves to me through art-making. Yet, as the methods I utilize in the studio are a conduit for these inquiries, so is the examination of transference, information loss and facade implicit in the work through the very techniques employed in its creation.

Settling the Estate
Acrylic, ink, Okawara on panel
38 x 36", 2018

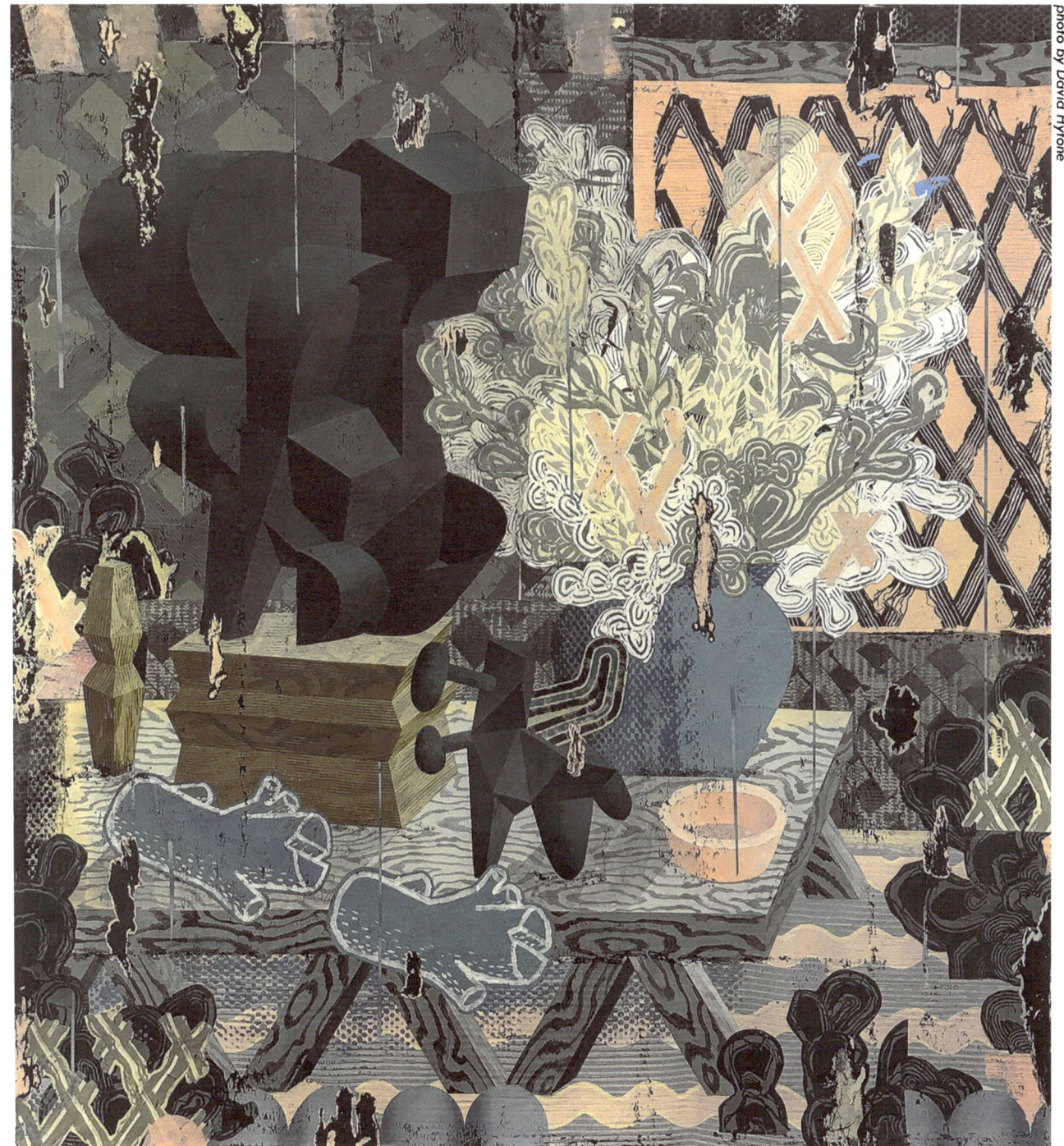

photo by David Hytone

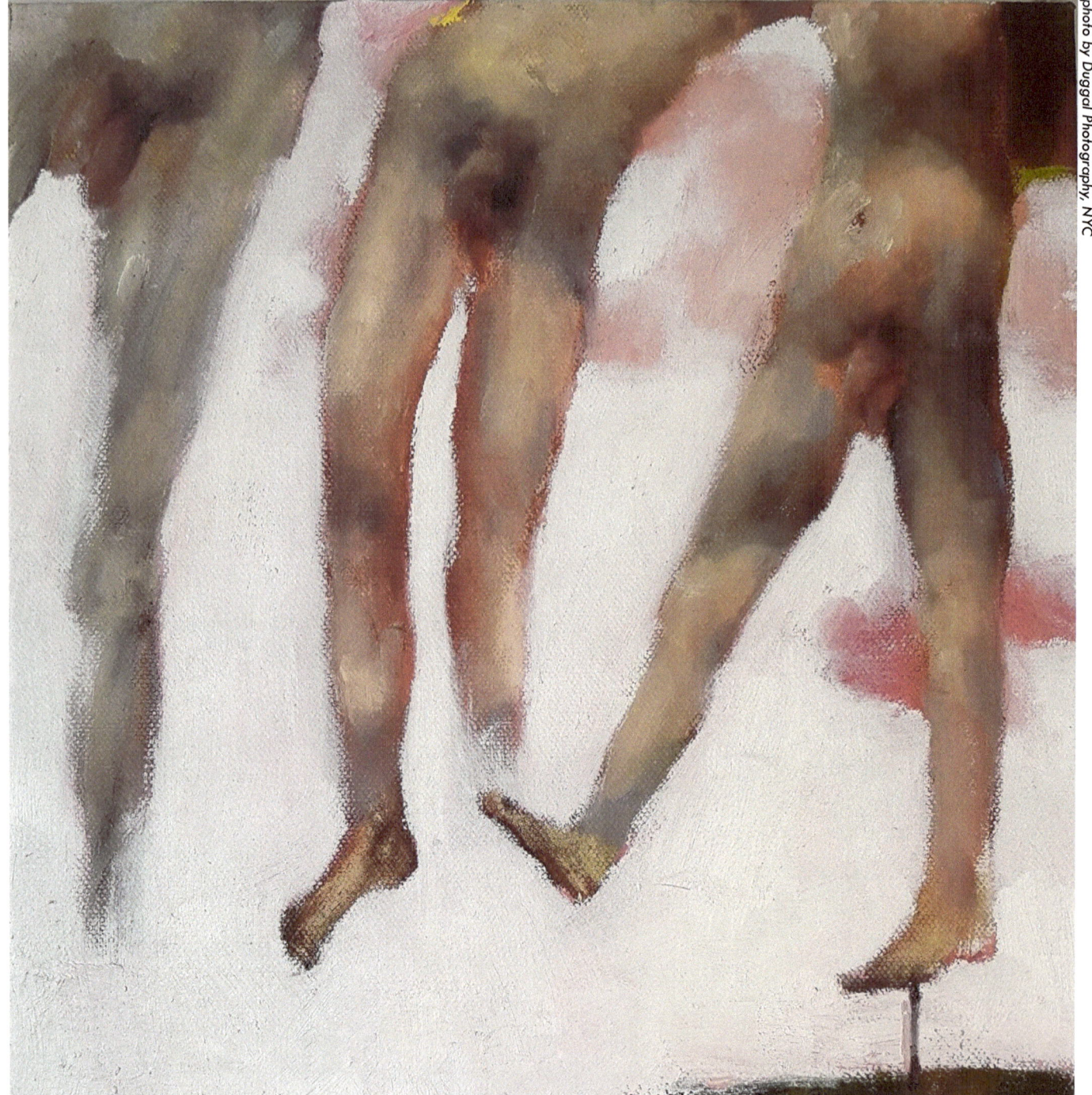

photo by Duggal Photography, NYC

Karen Kaapcke
Center on Contemporary Art

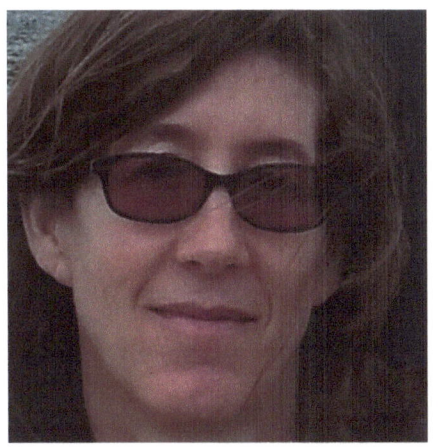

Karen Kaapcke

"A painting is like a house. Within its architecture, previously homeless narratives and metaphors can take shelter."

I am story-minded, and work largely with the figure; I trusts the image that emerges, allowing it to remain as raw material as I craft the narrative.

"I work to form a narrative that has no literal meaning but rather one that relies on a feeling of physical space, as if it were in a poem, a metaphor, or a dream."

I crowd or disperse my subjects into funnelled corners, or cavernous rooms, raising or pitching their foundations so that they seem at any minute to fall off the canvas or remain in their space for an undetermined time. My relationship with the edge of the canvas is historical; I hold the tradition of painting in view as an edge, pushing and pulling at the tradition to contain and at the same time open up, the narrative.

Born in New York City, Karen began painting and drawing while completing her Masters degree in Philosophy. She then studied at the Art Students League in New York City, the Ecole Albert Defois in France, and at the National Academy of Design where she won a full scholarship.

Karen has taught with Parsons School of Design, the Crosby Street Painting Studio, and currently teaches privately out of her studio. She is also the founder and director of the Young Urban Artists - a drawing and painting workshop for teens in New York City.

Karen has exhibited extensively, both in galleries and in museums such as The Butler Institute and Fontbonne University. She has been the recipient of many awards for her work including a first place award from the Portrait Society of America, and is in private collections throughout the country and in Europe. Her work has been written about in the Huffington Post, Poets & Artists Magazine, International Artists Magazine, Professional Artist Magazine and Fine Art Connoisseur among others. Most recently Karen created the paintings for and co-produced Life's Stages: A Collaboration, a unique painting and musical collaboration that had its NYC premiere at The National Opera Center.

Karen and her family currently share their time between her home and studio in New York City and in France. You can view more of her work at karenkaapcke.weebly.com and for information about the Young Urban Artists program visit urbanartistsacademy.weebly.com

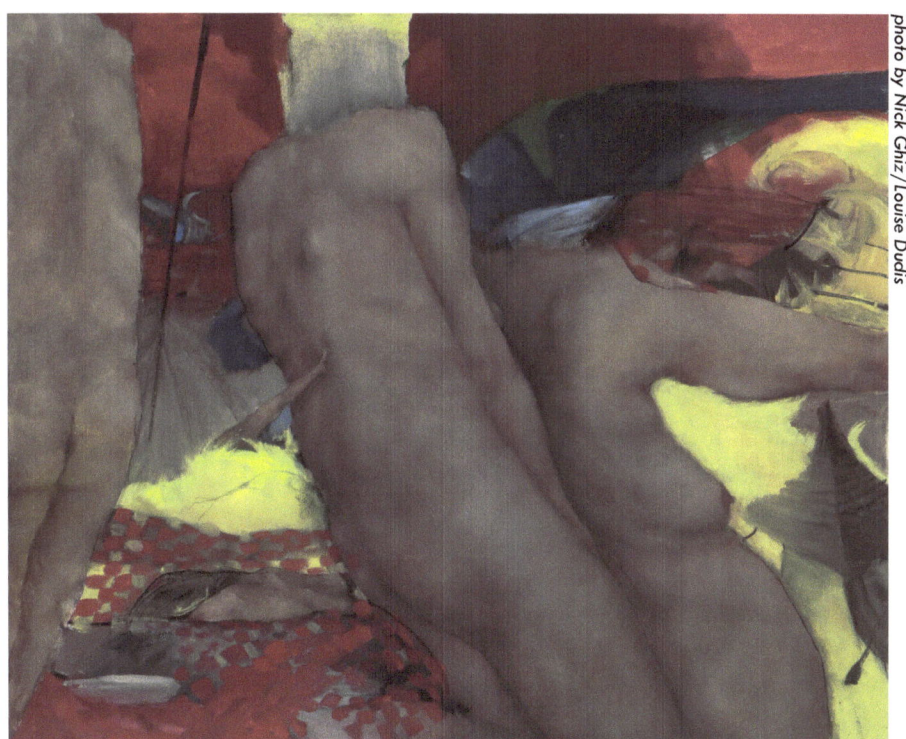

photo by Nick Ghiz/Louise Dudis

Arc en Ciel
Oil on Canvas, 10 x 10", 2017

Elle Capitaine (Raft V)
Oil on Canvas, 24 x 30", 2018

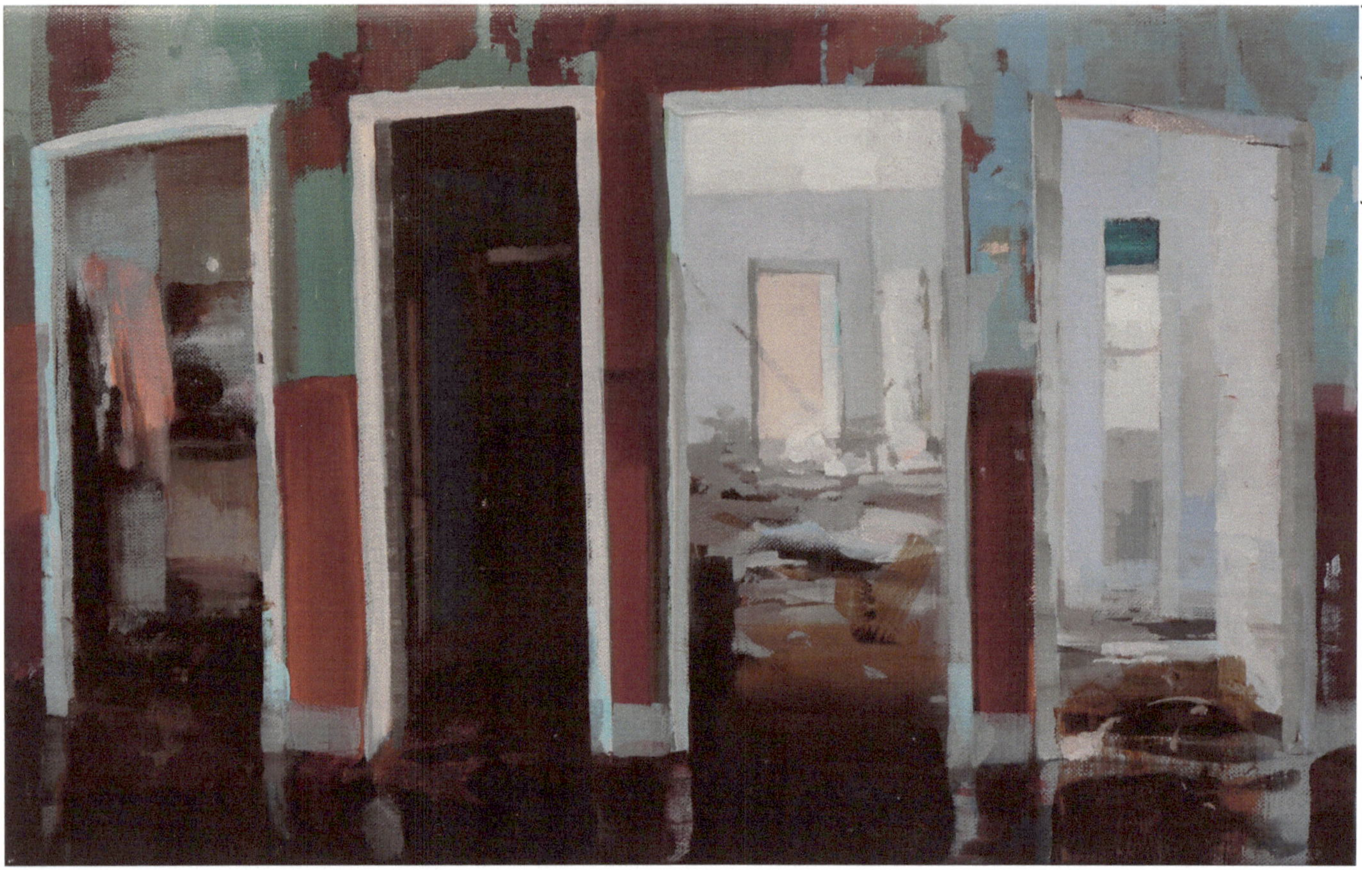

photos by Alex Kanevsky

Four Doors
Oil on linen, 11 x 18", 2017

Alex Kanevsky

Alex Kanevsky was born in Russia in 1963. He studied mathematics at Vilnius University in Lithuania before coming to the United States. After his arrival to Philadelphia in 1983 he worked as Russian translator, illustrator at the Psychiatric Nursing Magazine and drew pictures for the telephone book advertisements. After attending PAFA (1989-93) and winning a Pew Fellowship (1997) he devoted himself to painting full time. Alex Kanevsky lives and works in Philadelphia and New Hampshire. He has exhibited his work in the United States, Canada, Italy, UK, France and Ireland.

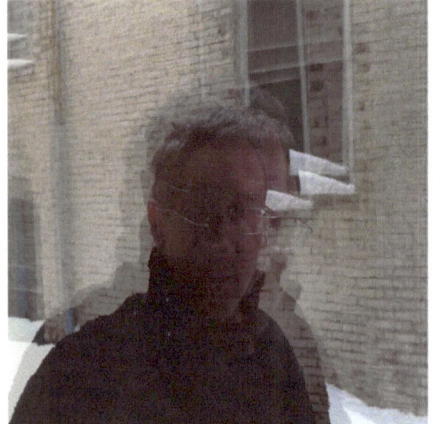

"An artist attempts to create a language, foreign to all but himself, and then say a few things in that language in such a way that would make them clear to anybody who listens, even if the language remains foreign to them."

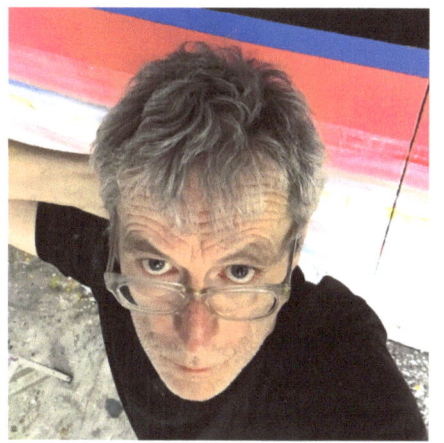

"My current paintings don't really lend themselves to statements. They don't deliberately "reference" anything nor do they address "issues" (art or otherwise). They simply exist as what they are: objects/images that occupy space on a wall, and, hopefully, in your eyes and mind and perhaps your gut."

Ken Kelly

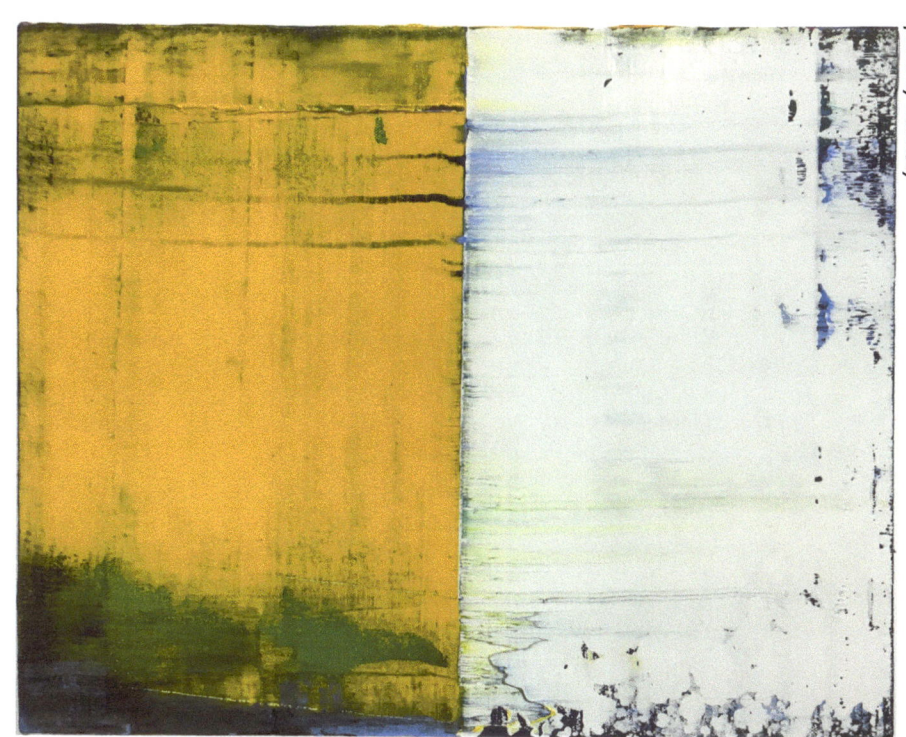

photo by Ken Kelly

I was born in Magnolia, Arkansas in 1955, and grew up there and in other small towns in the very deep South. I arrived in Seattle in 1981 by way of an unfinished stint in graduate school in Arizona and have been a Seattle-based painter for my entire professional career. I will probably remain so until the very end. This exhibit will be my third with CoCA, going all the way back to 1985 with the "Neo York/Seattle" show.

Untitled 03
Oil on canvas, 11 x 14", 2018

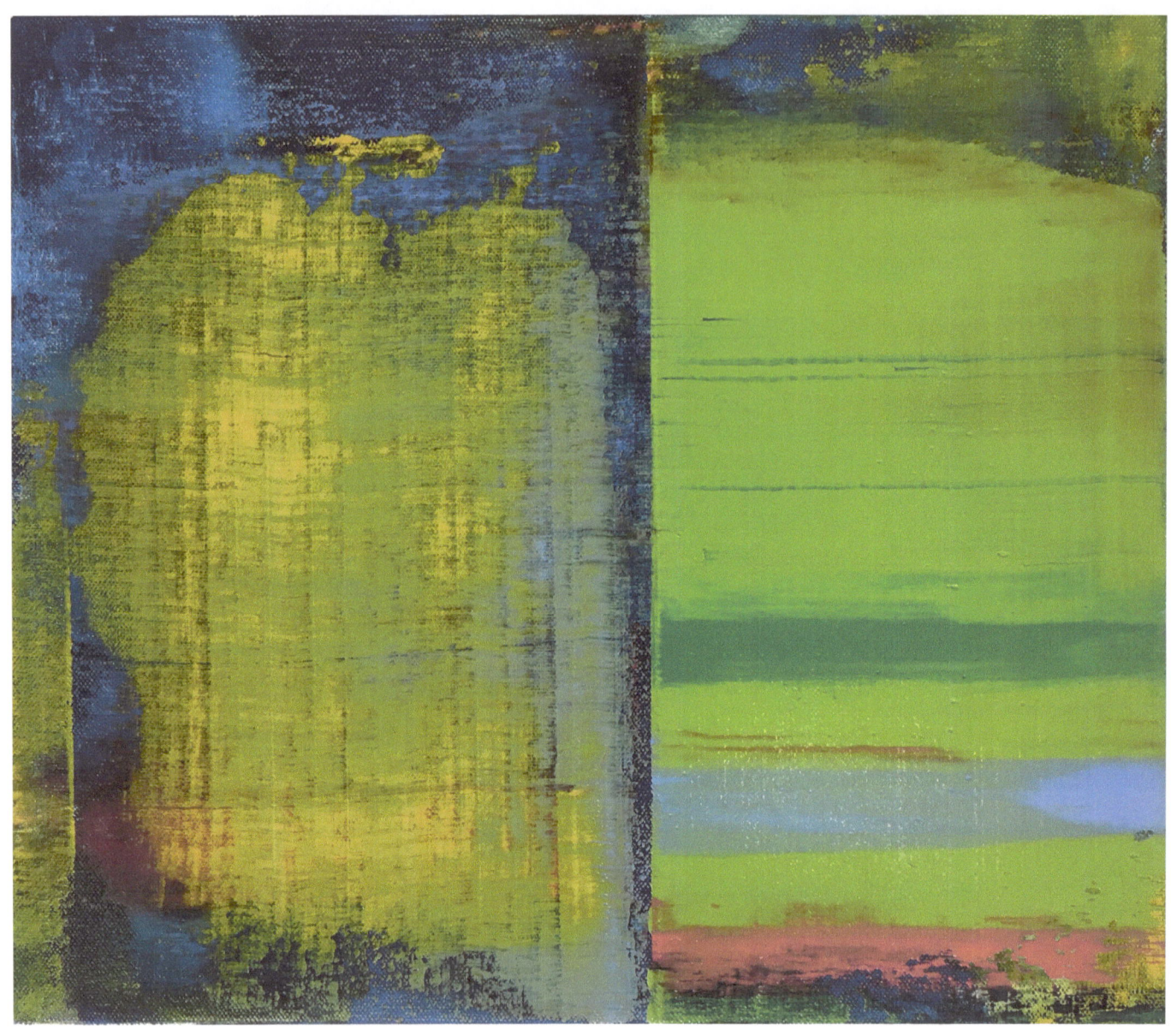

Untitled 01
Oil on canvas, 10 x 12", 2018

Painters Who Fucking Know How to Paint   Center on Contemporary Art

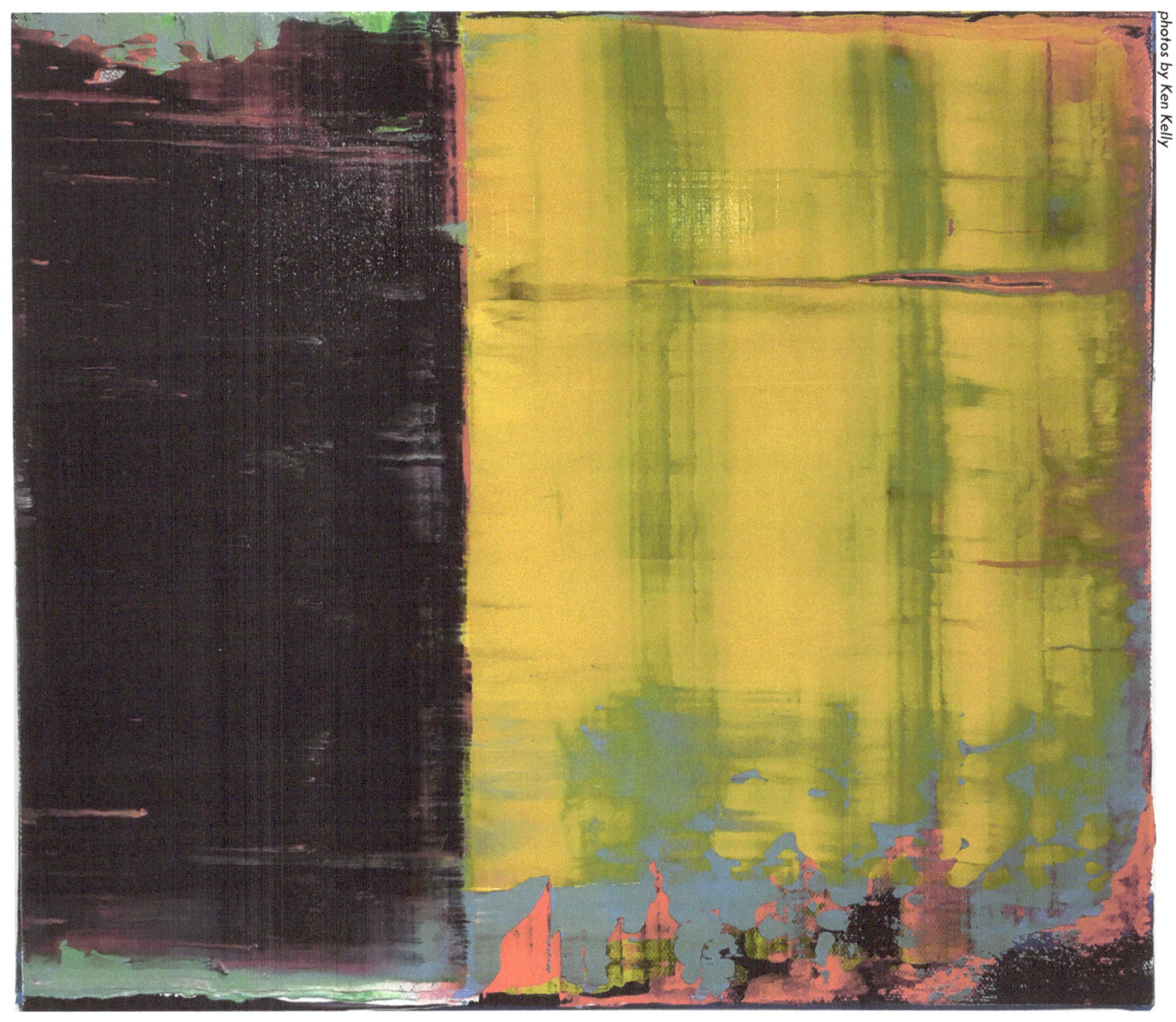

photos by Ken Kelly

Untitled 02
Oil on canvas, 10 x 12", 2018

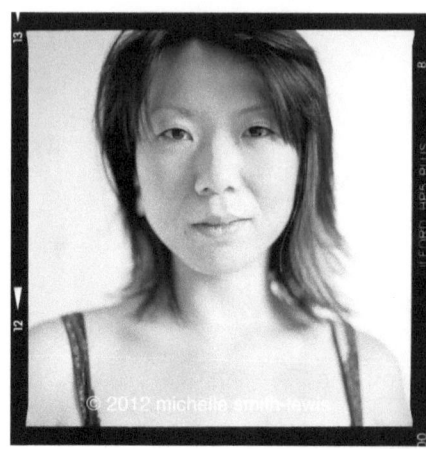
© 2012 michelle smith-lewis

Kathy Liao

Kathy Liao currently resides in Kansas City, MO, and teaches at Missouri Western State University as the Director of the Painting and Printmaking Studio Art Program. Drawing inspirations from her diverse cultural background and personal history, Kathy Liao mixed media work is about the intimate yet universal concept of relationships. Liao received her MFA in Painting from Boston University and BFA in Painting and Drawing from University of Washington, Seattle. Liao is a recipient of various awards including the StudiosINC Studio Residency Program, Charlotte Street Foundation Studio Residency, Elizabeth Greenshield Foundation Grant, Artist Grants from Anderson Ranch Arts Center, Vermont Studio Center, and Jentel Artist Residency. In the past, Liao taught at Boston University, University of Washington, Seattle University, and Gage Academy of Art. Her work was shown in Boston, New York, Los Angeles, Seattle, Kansas City, and many other cities nationally and internationally.

I think a lot about the distance we experience around us. There are some distances that seem so impossibly far out of reach. In our iPhone-staring, social media fueled world right now, one can be right next to another and feels a million miles apart. Then there are moments when we experience an intimate connection, whether through physical touch or compressed onto the same screen during FaceTime calls.

My recent paintings are a record of an experience, a feeling. In a familiar space, both the presence and the absence of figure are equally palpable. A portrait may begin with the person sitting in front of me or a transient smile over FaceTime, and all that might get buried under layers of painted recollection of how the sun felt the day he sat there. My mixed media work is painted from observations, layered with sharp and hazy memories and recorded snapshot photos. With each painting, I am constantly re-establishing my relationship with the subject matter, being conscientious of my distance to them, physically and emotionally.

I project my thought and my experiences onto the canvas and the image pushes back. The result is an intimate back and forth conversation between myself and the work. The dialogue goes through stages of cutting and pasting painted paper and reclaimed scraps, and spills over to a physical pushing, dragging, and dripping of thickly-laid and scraped-away paint. In the end, there may be so much on the painting, or only traces of history left visible.

"With each painting, I am constantly re-establishing my relationship with the subject matter, being conscientious of my distance to them, physically and emotionally. I project my thought and my experiences onto the canvas and the image pushes back."

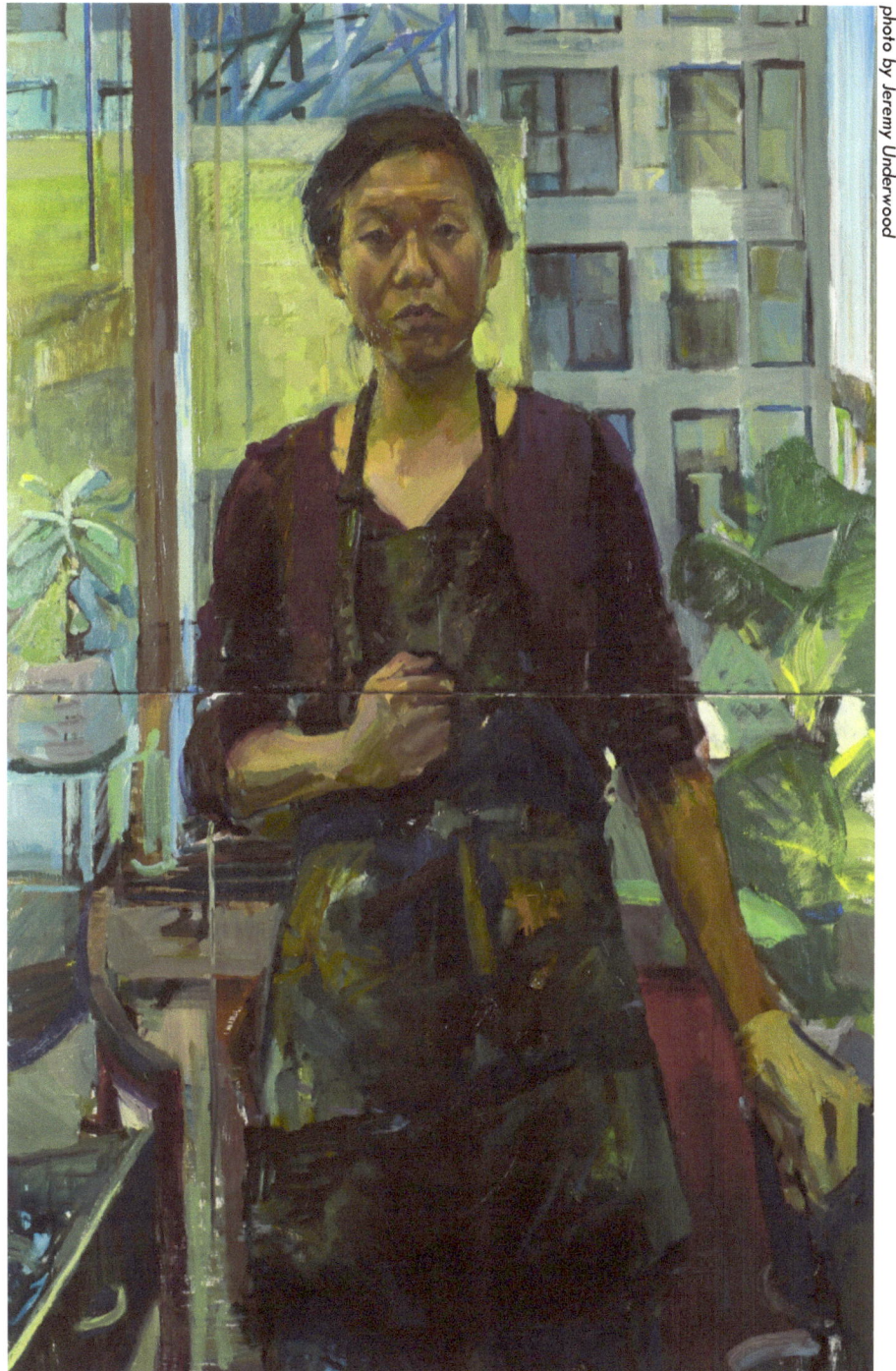

photo by Jeremy Underwood

Self Portrait KCMO
Oil on canvas, 60 x 48", 2017

Kathy Liao

"Gravity and its direct somatic link to the body dominate the trajectory of my recent work... Most important to me is the experimental nature of their origins – pushing acrylic paint to do what it's not supposed to do."

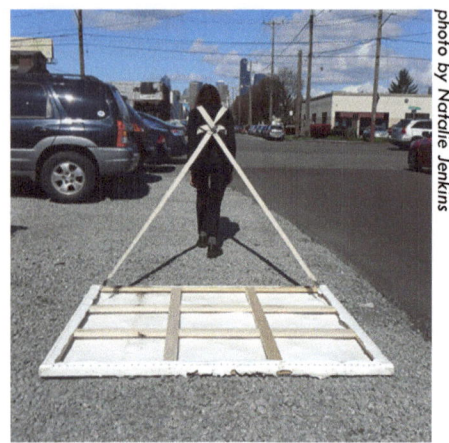

photo by Natalie Jenkins

Margie Livingston

"Too Soon for Hindsight"

"Gravity is a sweet taste of mortality and our strength to resist it, a luxuriating in the pull of the earth and the pull of muscles against it..." writes Rebecca Solnit in A Field Guide to Getting Lost. Gravity and its direct somatic link to the body dominate the trajectory of my recent work. The distance between stacking planks made out of paint, draping sheets of paint on a peg, and dragging a painting down the street may at first glance seem vast, but they are connected in multiple ways. All these works reveal the force of gravity and the patina of time as if they were actual living flesh. Moreover, there's my frequent material: "skins," of acrylic paint, rolled, cut, draped, or tacked onto stretchers. Most important to me is the experimental nature of their origins – pushing acrylic paint to do what it's not supposed to do – a quest that has dominated my work since 2009.

Dragging a painting down the street marks the surface with the pull of gravity – a record of getting from point A to point B. In 1979 Barbara Rose wrote of "Painting's capacity to materialize an image."* Although this description could apply to the Dragged Paintings, more precisely, they embody the image of their making. The marked surface records the strain of my muscles, the resistance of their faces against the earth.

The first impulse for these new performative works was to harm a painting so I could examine the potential of mending. Enacting the gesture, I found the content transformed into a study of guilt and shame. When I pass people on the street while dragging a painting, I feel more like the Log Lady from Twin Peaks than an artist. Sometimes I just put my head down, so my hat hides my face, and try to ignore that passersby cross the street to avoid me. Other times I take someone with me, as if to demonstrate that what I'm doing is worthy. Some days I just can't face putting on the harness and going out in public.

These new working methods also connect me to art historical influences. I love how the act of dragging a painting invokes Harold Rosenburg's term, "Action Painting" thereby connecting me to Jackson Pollock and Willem de Kooning. The violence of that action brings to mind Christian Marclay's 1999 "Guitar Drag," which was made after James Byrd Jr., a 49-year-old black man, was dragged to death by white supremacists.

Art history connects me to these macho gestures but my quest is for something more personal: a meditation on entropy, aging, and death.

I live with the discomfort of not knowing. Not knowing where the work is going. Not knowing how to reconcile the darkness with the comic gesture of dragging a painting. Incorporating the dark as well as the light, the guilt, the risk of going too far, being too serious one minute, and silly the next, living with the collage of disparate parts that makes up my practice. I may not know where this is going, but I'm curious about what I'll find.

*Barbara Rose, American Painting: the Eighties, Buffalo: Thorny-Sidney Press, 1979.

photo by Richard Nicol

Margie Livingston is a painter using diverse means to reflect on the weight of painting's cultural hegemony, the limits of her media, and her artistic forbearers.

Based in Seattle, she earned her M.F.A. in painting from the University of Washington. Her awards include the Arts Innovator Award in 2010; the Neddy Fellowship in 2010; the Betty Bowen Annual Memorial Award in 2006; and a Fulbright Scholarship in 2001. Livingston's work resides in the permanent collections of the Shenzhen Fine Art Institute, the Seattle Art Museum, King County, the City of Seattle, the Portland Art Museum, and the Henry Art Gallery.

Her 2016 video, "Dragging a Painting," was supported by the Seattle Art Museum, where it is currently on view. The Portland Art Museum presented her solo exhibition in 2015. She is represented by Luis De Jesus Los Angeles and Greg Kucera in Seattle.

She is preparing new works for an exhibition in September of 2018 at Greg Kucera Gallery. In 2017, the Jacob Lawrence Gallery at the University of Washington invited her to present "Artel," in which six people wore an artist-made harness to drag a painting across the campus, considering the violence of production, collective action, and chance.

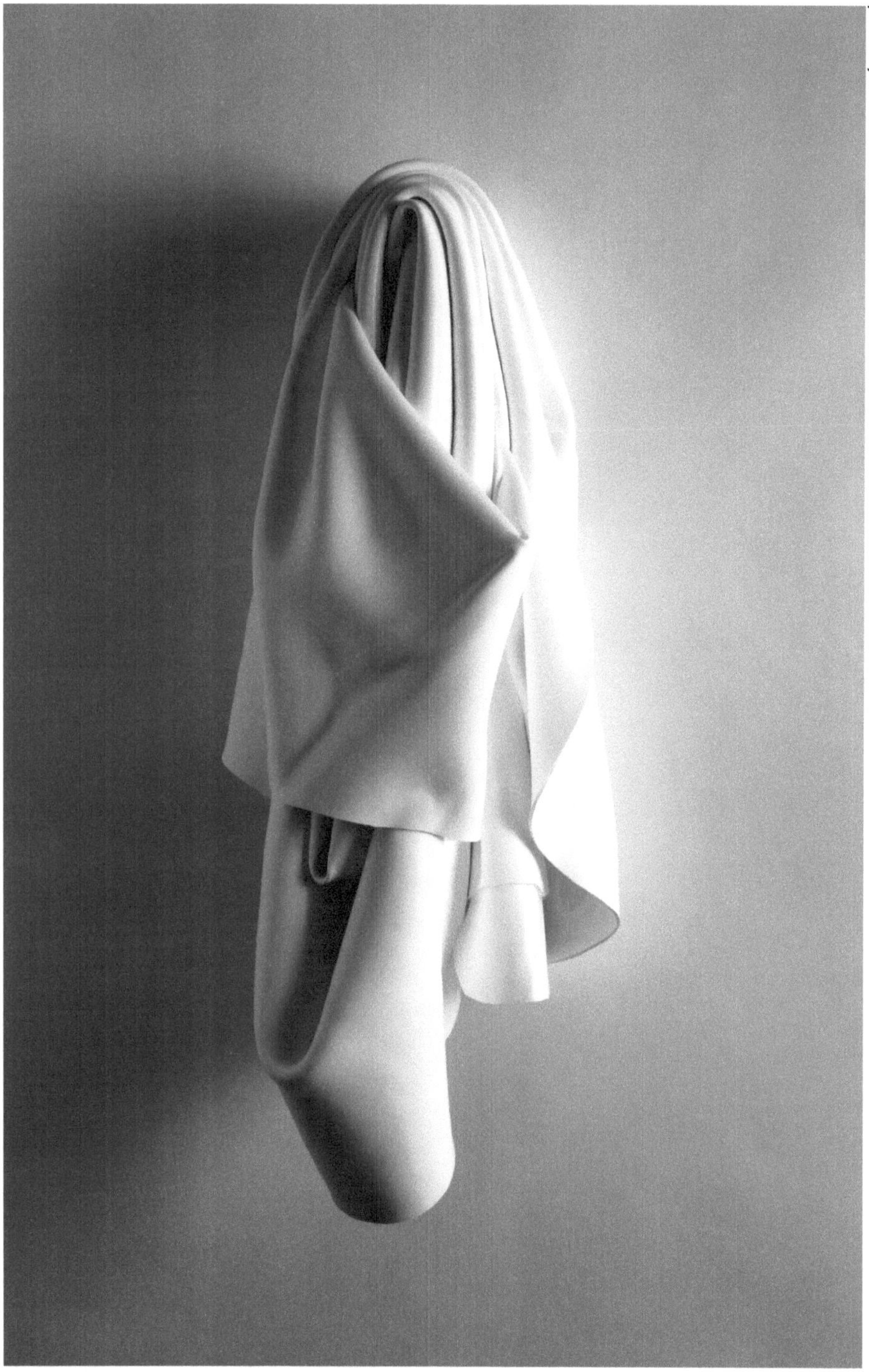

Draped Painting #12
Acrylic paint on wooden peg
23 x 8 x 8.5", 2014

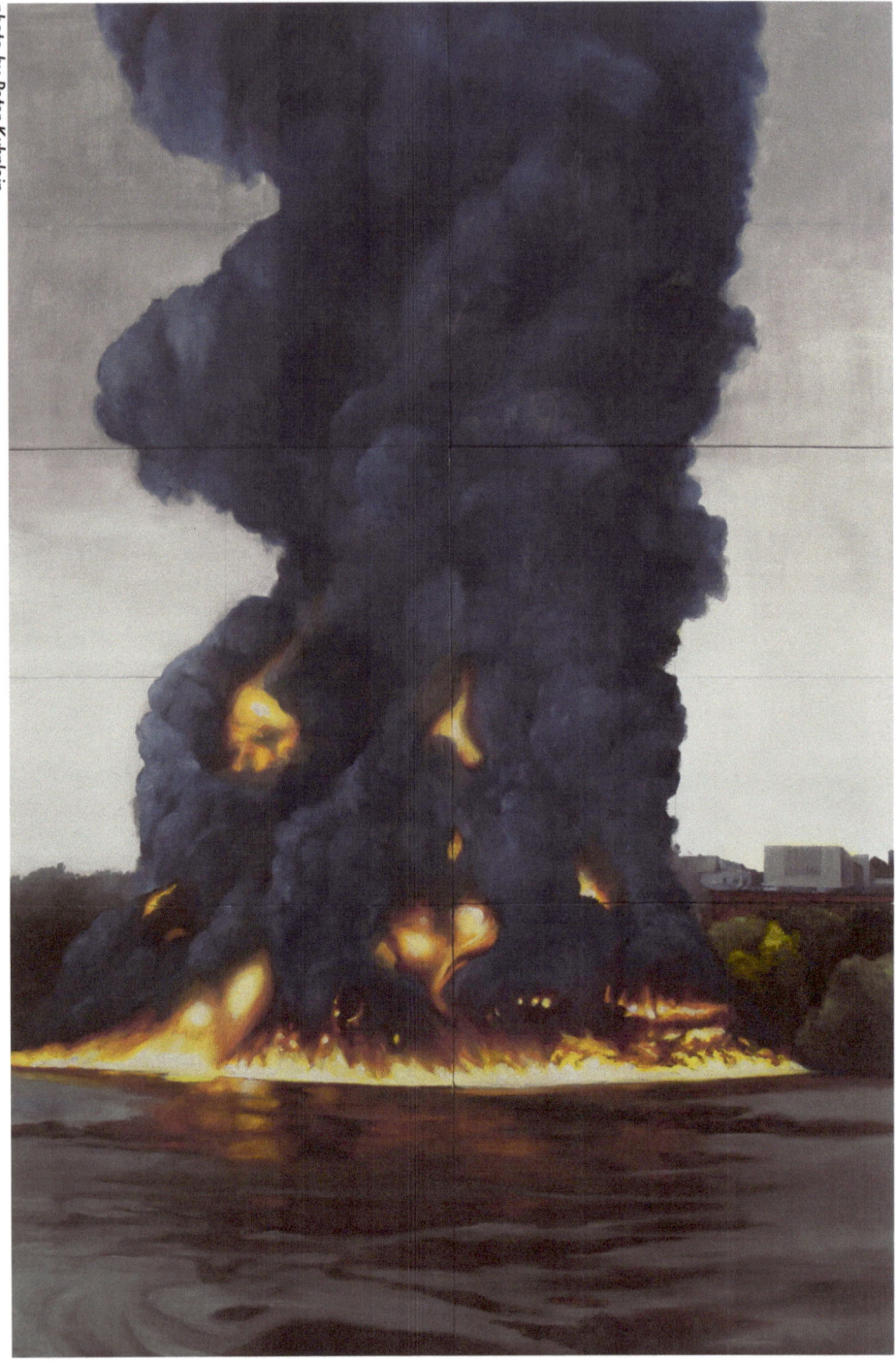

photo by Peter Kuhnlein

"It is this disconnect between our collective actions and their consequences that fuel this body of work. But as a painter, I can't deny the attraction of the beauty inherent in a massive release of energy. The explosions, though horrific in their implications, are intrinsically beautiful when captured as a moment, and I find it impossible to look away."

Natalie Niblack is a visual artist working in drawing, oil painting, printmaking and ceramics. She lives on the Skagit River on Fir Island. From this viewpoint, she is able to observe the pressure of conflicting demands on a fragile landscape. This environment of beauty, conflict and change has increasingly informed her artwork since moving to Skagit Valley in 2000.

She taught visual art at Shoreline Community College from 1996 to 2016. She received an MFA from Edinburgh College of Art in Scotland in 1993. She has shown her work in solo and group shows internationally, nationally and regionally.

Lynchburg
Oil on wood panels
36 x 24", 2016

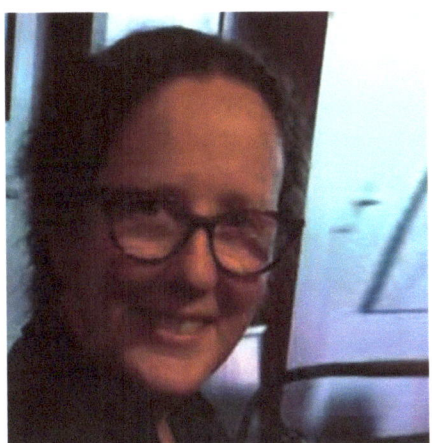

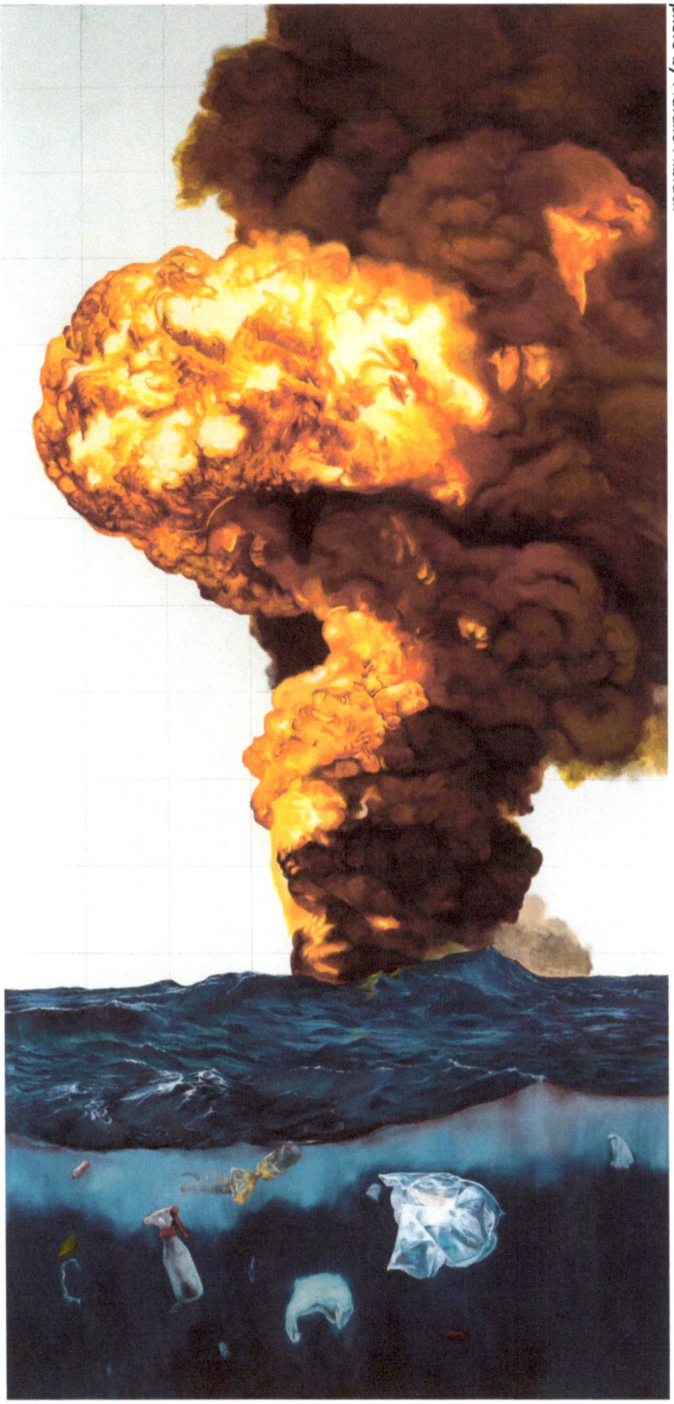

photo by Natalie Niblack

Natalie Niblack

This work reflects a pervading sense in accelerated change in our culture- change in the climate, environment, politics, and war. Everything in the world around us is impacted by human activity, if not in itself man-made. In this work, I attempt to recognize that the landscape we see everyday is a result of the choices we all have made and participate in. I drive, use plastics in almost every product I come into contact with, I eat foods from every ocean and continent, and I create waste; the landscape I see is filled with roads, cars, power lines, dikes, smokestacks, and farm equipment. And though I participate in an economy built around disposable products, I also see and read about the ocean filling with micro-plastics, oil spills, and pipeline explosions. I live near a major railway for oil and coal, and I read about the fossil fuel industry and its attendant callous disregard for the environment, when broken pipelines and devastated watersheds are an acceptable risk, simply collateral damage. It is this disconnect between our collective actions and their consequences that fuel this body of work. It asks the viewer to recognize the consequences of our relationship with the environment, and that the choices we have collectively made is inevitable, and perhaps irrevocably, altering the world around us. But as a painter, I can't deny the attraction of the beauty inherent in a massive release of energy. The explosions, though horrific in their implications, are intrinsically beautiful when captured as a moment, and I find it impossible to look away.

Watershed
Oil and graphite
on canvas
96 x 46", 2017

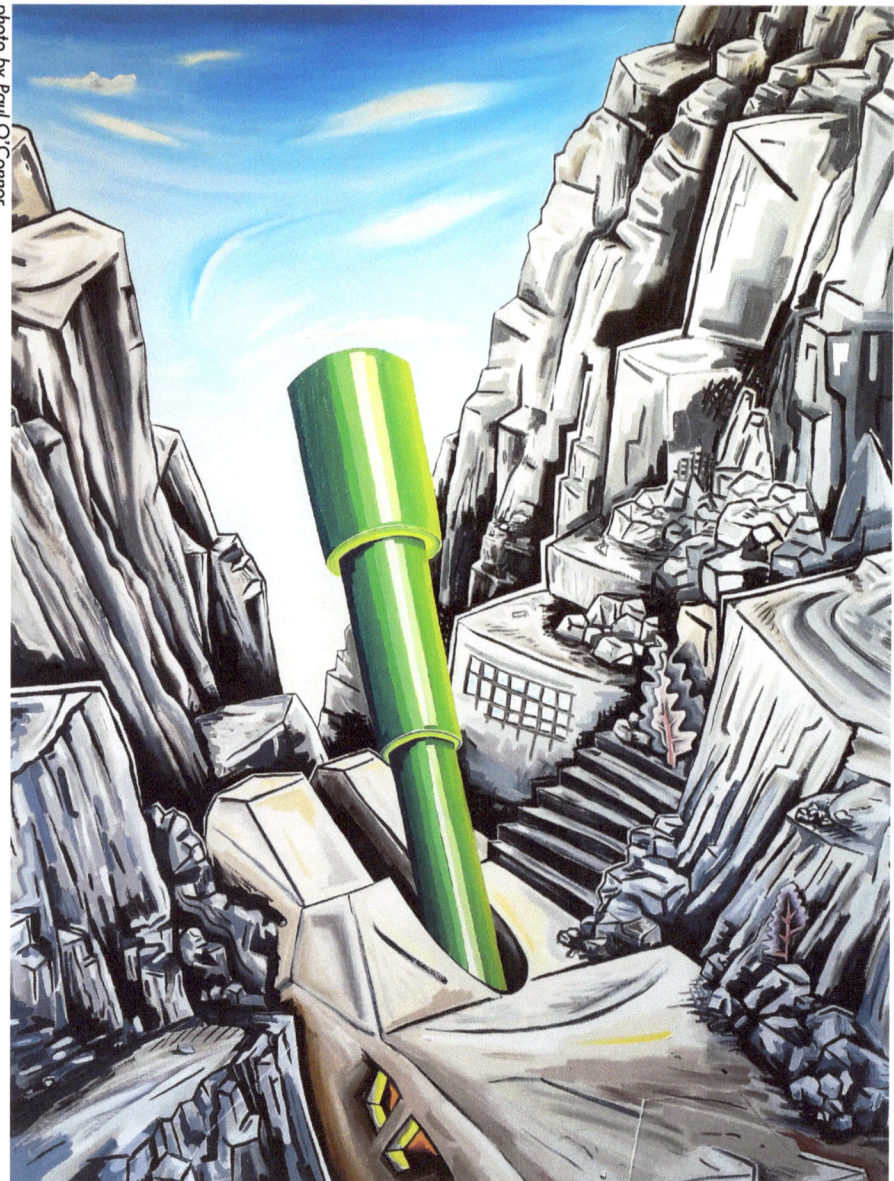

photo by Paul O'Connor

FLUXUS STATION
Oil on canvas, 57 x 70", 2015

Allan Packer

Allan Packer is known for his motorized, painted, shaped canvases in kinetic motion. As master printer for Dorset Fine Arts, he produced prints for Kananginak, Pitseolak and Pudlo Pudlat. He studied with Stanley William Hayter at Atelier 17 in Paris. Awards include Canada Council and Artist Trust grants. Residencies include Kohler Arts, Banff Centre for the Arts and the International Studio Curatorial Program. Packer exhibits internationally.

Growing up during the vestiges of the cold war and watching Hollywood espionage films like "Ice Station Zebra" – Fluxus station thrusts the telescope from the slit of the bunker searching for the moment that never comes. The bunker in the shape of a coyote pays homage to Fluxus member Joseph Beuys and his piece featuring a coyote "I Like America and America Likes Me".

photo by Izzy Schwartz

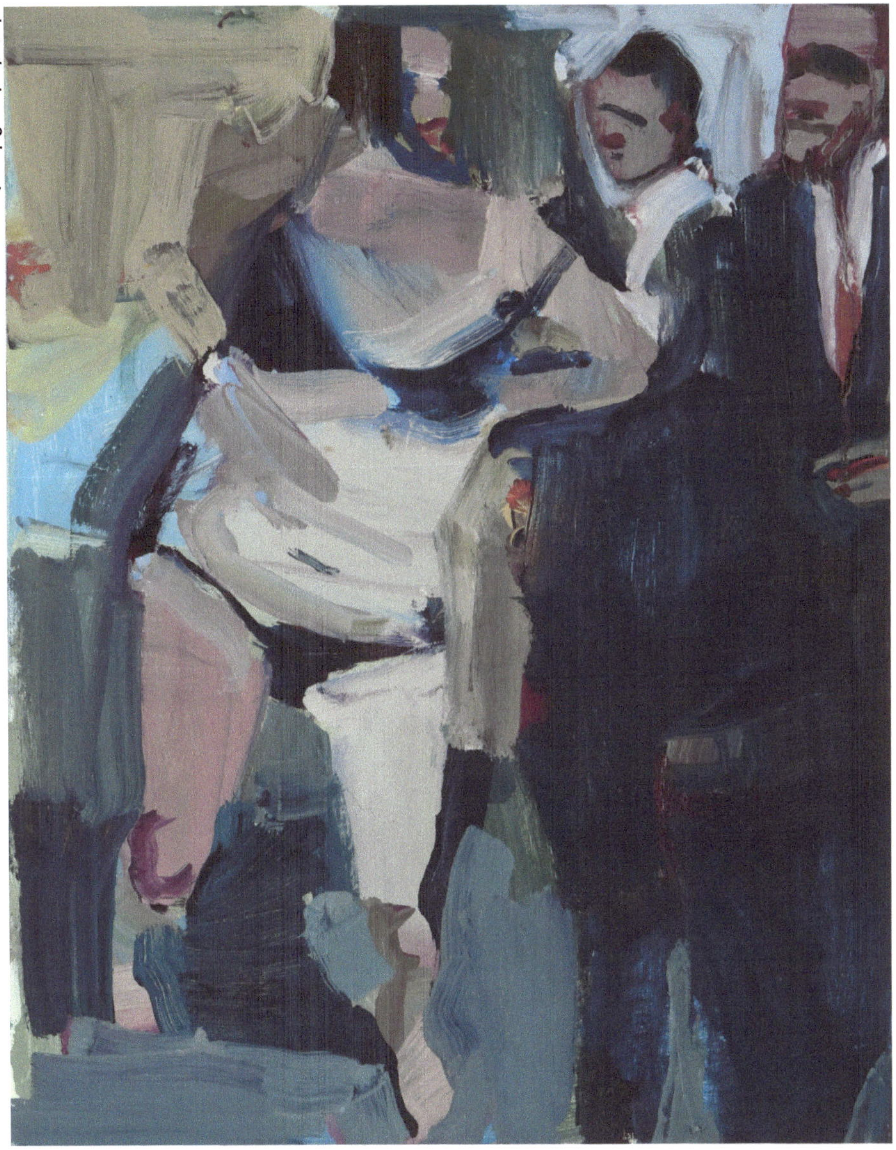

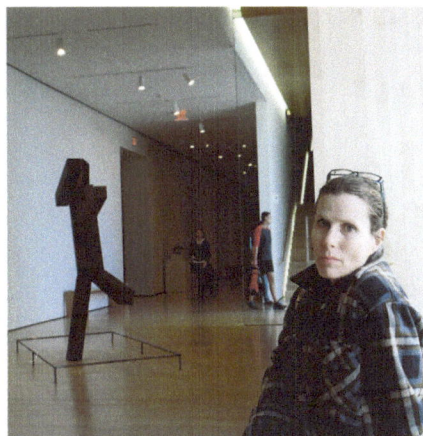

Jennifer Pochinski

My family moved to Hawaii when I was 11 years old. I remember falling in love with this place that was so new. Haole is the Hawaiian word for foreigner. For some reason I felt oddly comfortable with this term. After receiving my BFA from the University of Hawaii in 1991, I spent the subsequent years being a Haole in other parts of the world. I have spent extended periods in Germany, London, Greece and even the East Coast and now California, where I live since 2010.

On Green Street
Oil on panel, 16 x 20", 2018

The figure is the central focus of my work - but it merely a vehicle to move paint.

Being a very painterly painter has its pitfalls. I feel I must keep on my toes. It is easy to be seduced by the mark and find myself in a swirl of cliches. On the flip side, I oftentimes find myself trying to 'get it right' What happens in-between these two tendencies is what I call painting.

"Being a very painterly painter has its pitfalls. I feel I must keep on my toes. It is easy to be seduced by the mark and find myself in a swirl of cliches. On the flip side, I oftentimes find myself trying to 'get it right' What happens in-between these two tendencies is what I call painting."

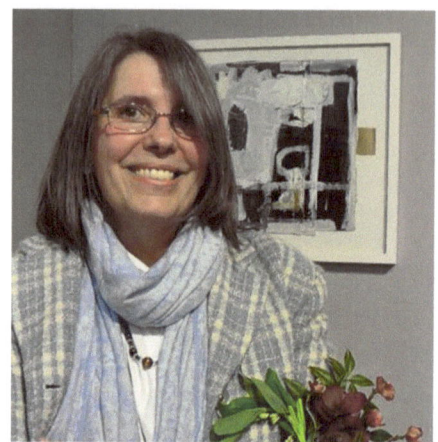

Flora Ramirez-Bustamante

Flora Ramírez-Bustamante grew up in Madrid, Spain. She is a linguist and an artist. As a young adult, she lived and studied in Madrid, Barcelona (Spain) and Athens (Greece). She emigrated to the United States in 2001 and currently lives in the Seattle area. Ramírez- Bustamante has participated in two artists and group exhibitions in Seattle, Oregon and Hawaii.

My interests as an artist encompass inquiries and reflections on the creative process and the experimental use of materials. My work shows a delicate balance between my intellectual interests in linguistics, poetry, culture, abstraction and myself as a reference of exploration. My method in working is process and materials oriented in that I don't limit my field of actions. Not constraining my options regarding materials, processes and goals, I discover possibilities and a sense of freedom in creating.

During my studio practice, I embrace imperfection, accidents and the inspiration that this energy transpires.

"My interests as an artist encompass inquiries and reflections on the creative process and the experimental use of materials."

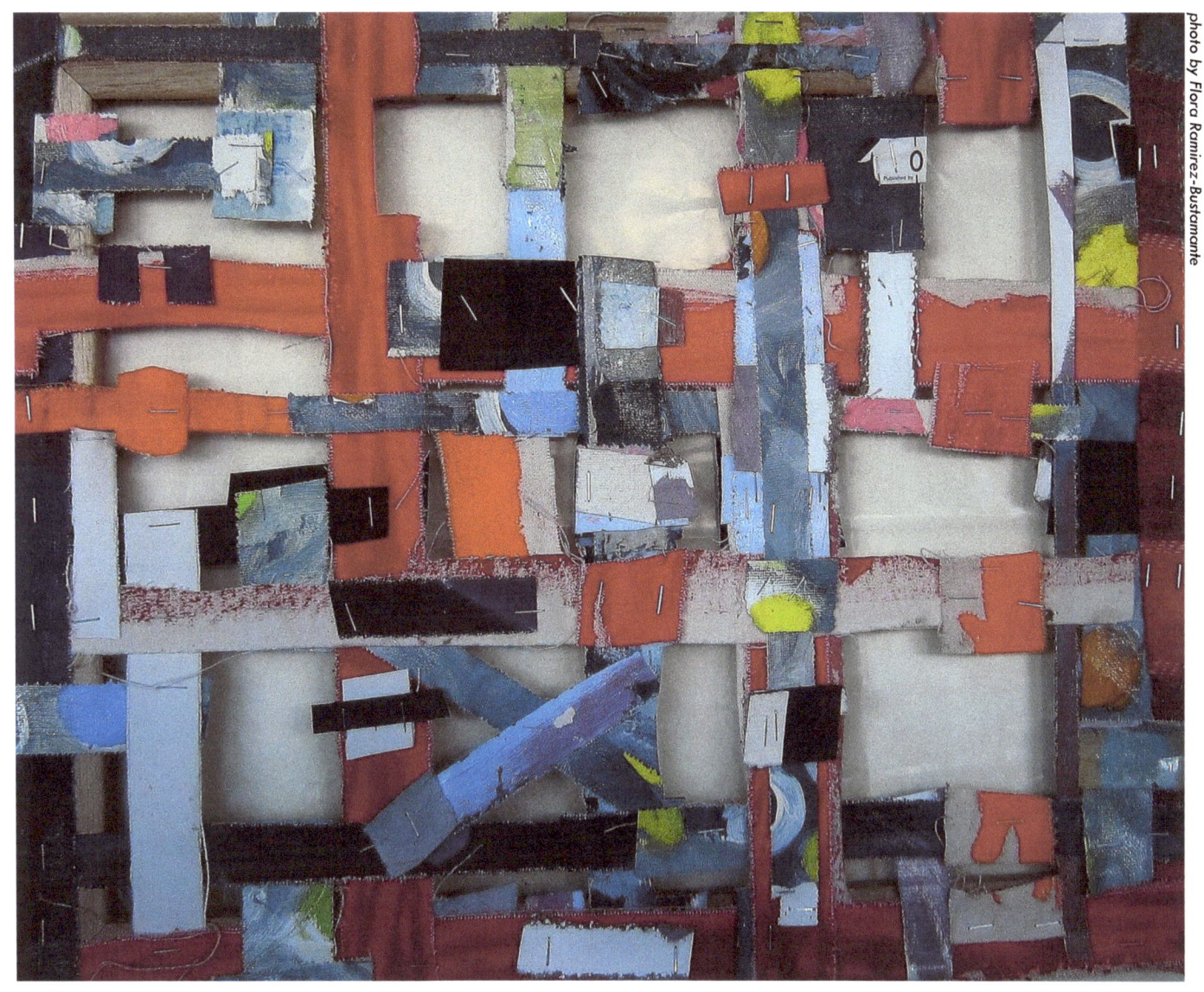

photo by Flora Ramirez-Bustamante

An Old Fabric In Red
Recycled oil painted canvas, fabric, other recycled materials and staples on a canvas frame, 15.5 x 20", 2018

Center on Contemporary Art   Flora Ramirez-Bustamante

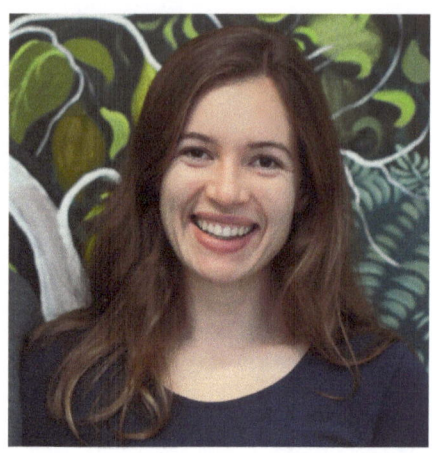

Adrianne Smits

Adrianne Smits is a painter and an ecologist. She graduated from Yale University in 2010 with a double major in Biology and Art, and received a PhD in Aquatic Science from University of Washington in Seattle in 2016. Her paintings derive from her experiences on long field expeditions into wilderness areas in Alaska, Washington, and California. She lived and maintained a studio practice in Seattle from 2011- 2016, and continues to show work in galleries and museums in the Pacific Northwest. She now lives in central California, drawing inspiration from landscapes along the pacific rim.

As an ecologist, I spend months at a time conducting scientific studies, allowing me unique access to remote places that in turn inspire my paintings. Any theme I pursue in a series of work stems from these initial outdoor observations. I use only a few sketches made on site to recall the memory and sensation of immersion in an ecosystem at a particular place and time. With such limited information, memories fade and warp – my larger studio compositions reflect this gradual untethering, growing exaggerated and flattened while retaining an immersive scale. I interpret and emphasize visual details from my encounters with nature in order to communicate the complexity of natural systems beyond their cursory picturesque value.

"I interpret and emphasize visual details from my encounters with nature in order to communicate the complexity of natural systems beyond their cursory picturesque value."

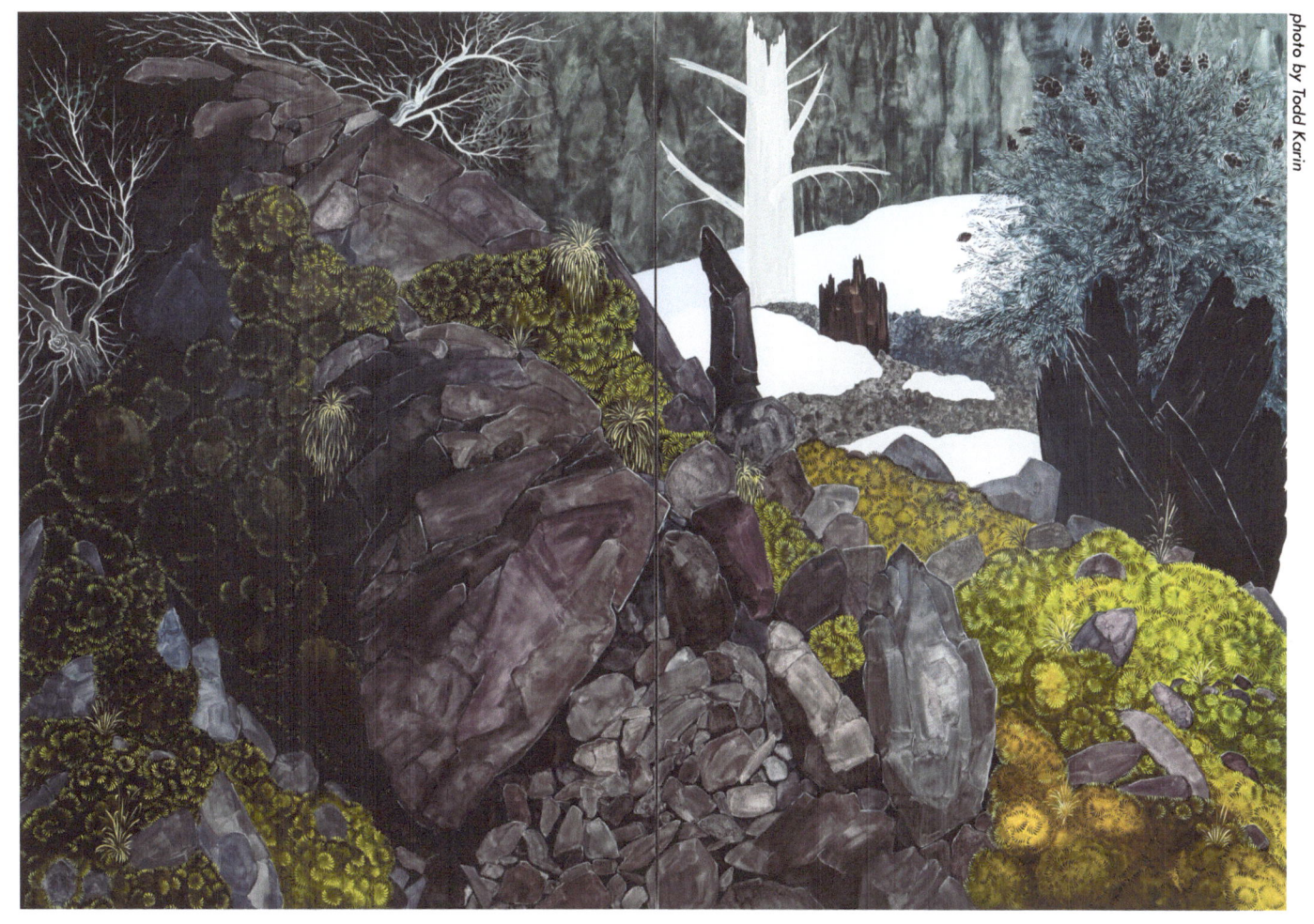

photo by Todd Karin

Franciscan Complex
Oil on canvas, diptych, 8.5 x 12.5', 2017

Center on Contemporary Art   Adrianne Smits

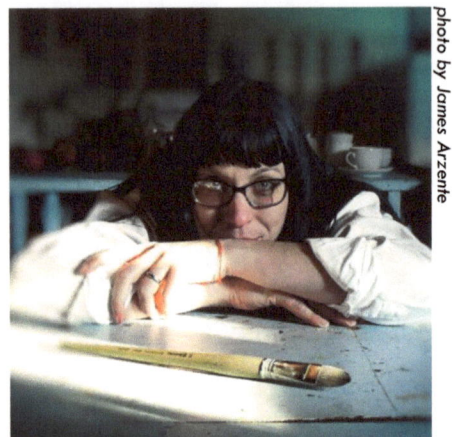

photo by James Arzente

Ruthie V.

Ruthie V. has exhibited work in the Bellevue Arts Museum, Tacoma Arts Museum, Bellingham Arts Museum, Smith & Vallee Gallery, Core Gallery, and others. She has a BA in painting from Western Washington University, and studied in Japan. In 2016 she started the Seattle Artist League, a community art school with a focus on drawing, painting, and printmaking.

Ruthie V. creates paintings that are direct, expressive, and carefully edited for simplicity. Always challenging herself to say more with less, she paints from observation, teasing out the essential form of her subject matter, a process that involves the viewer in the completion of an image. While allowing herself the freedom to paint diverse subject matter in a wide variety of styles, she frequently returns to, and sensitively renders, the human form.

Historically, I made paintings in as few sittings as possible, with minimal brush strokes, minimal materials, and minimal time - a practice acquired from my Japanese influences. In the last few years, I've shifted my restrictions, and invest more time into my paintings. I now layer many sittings and poses onto one canvas. While I prefer working from a live model, and I do so for drawings, my paintings take so much more time that photographs are necessary. With a camera in my hand, the model can be in motion. From a thousand photographs, I'll choose two or three, and layer them in transparent sheets. The transparent sheets give an empty look to the figure. I use a variety of transparent and opaque paints so I can occasionally reverse what is physical form, and what is emptiness. For me, emptiness can feel very full.

"I use a variety of transparent and opaque paints so I can occasionally reverse what is physical form, and what is emptiness. For me, emptiness can feel very full."

Painters Who Fucking Know How to Paint

Center on Contemporary Art

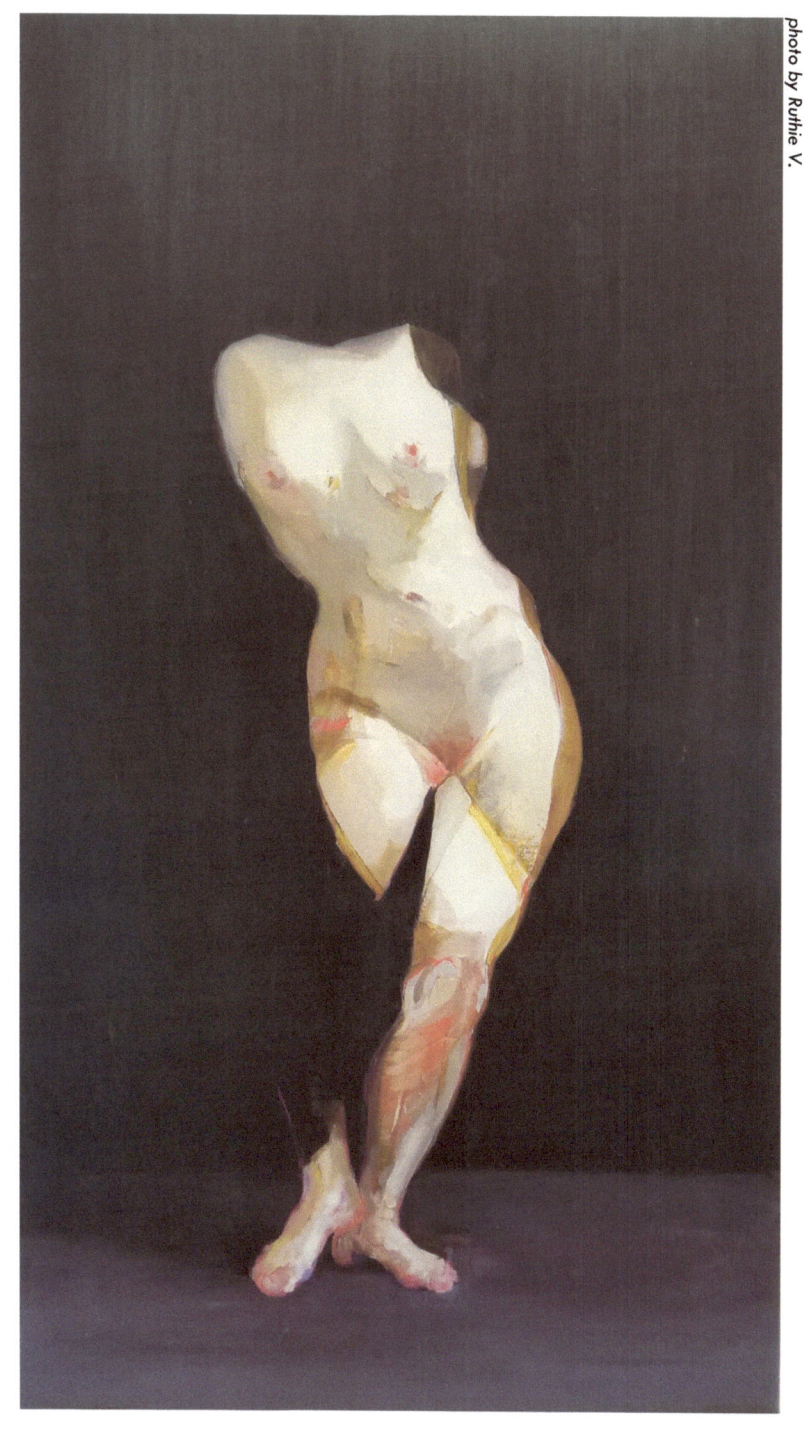

photo by Ruthie V.

Venus
Oil on linen, 72 x 42", 2018

Center on Contemporary Art

Ruthie V.

"I love color and use it without reservation. My work is sometimes described as childlike with a spontaneous and emotional appeal. I hope it looks easy but somehow it never is. It is always trial and error and always difficult to know when it is finished."

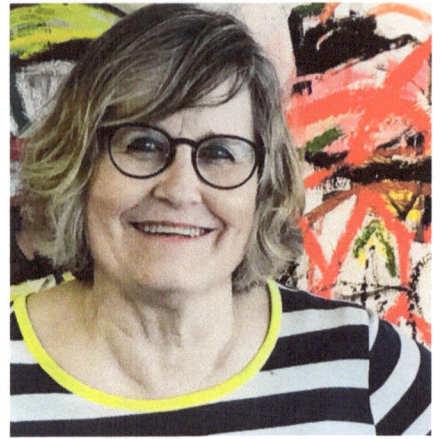

Paula Whelan

Paula Whelan is painter and mixed media artist who lives and works in Seattle, WA, where she shares a Tashiro Kaplan Building studio in Pioneer Square. Whelan grew up in Texas and received her MFA from the University of Texas, Austin. In her work she seeks to eliminate intentional representation. Whelan's work is not premeditated, and is not organized logically. She eliminates preconception and faces the canvas intuitively, curating the marks as she goes. Her spontaneous responses to the marks on the painting result in energetic and visually sophisticated works. Whelan has exhibited nationally including her 2015 solo exhibit at Cliff Gallery in Dallas, TX, SAM Gallery, Gallery 110, Bumbershoot and Portland Art Center. Her work is in numerous private and public collections including, Sellen, AIG, and The Container Store. www.paulawhelan.com

For some reason, I have always worked very intuitively. My most successful pieces usually share certain qualities or characteristics. Though I never work with any themes, many paintings or drawings could be described using words like energetic, bold, confrontational, assertive and graphic. Subtlety has never been my forte. I have always thought it was necessary to make a commitment to the space.

I find inspiration in everyday life, often a glimpse of a shape or color that I find arresting. It could be as simple as a spot of paint on the floor, a scrap of material, or a piece of styrofoam found in the trash. I love color and use it without reservation. My work is sometimes described as childlike with a spontaneous and emotional appeal. I hope it looks easy but somehow it never is. It is always trial and error and always difficult to know when it is finished. I keep hoping that will change and it will be more effortless but that day has never arrived.

photo by Paula Whelan

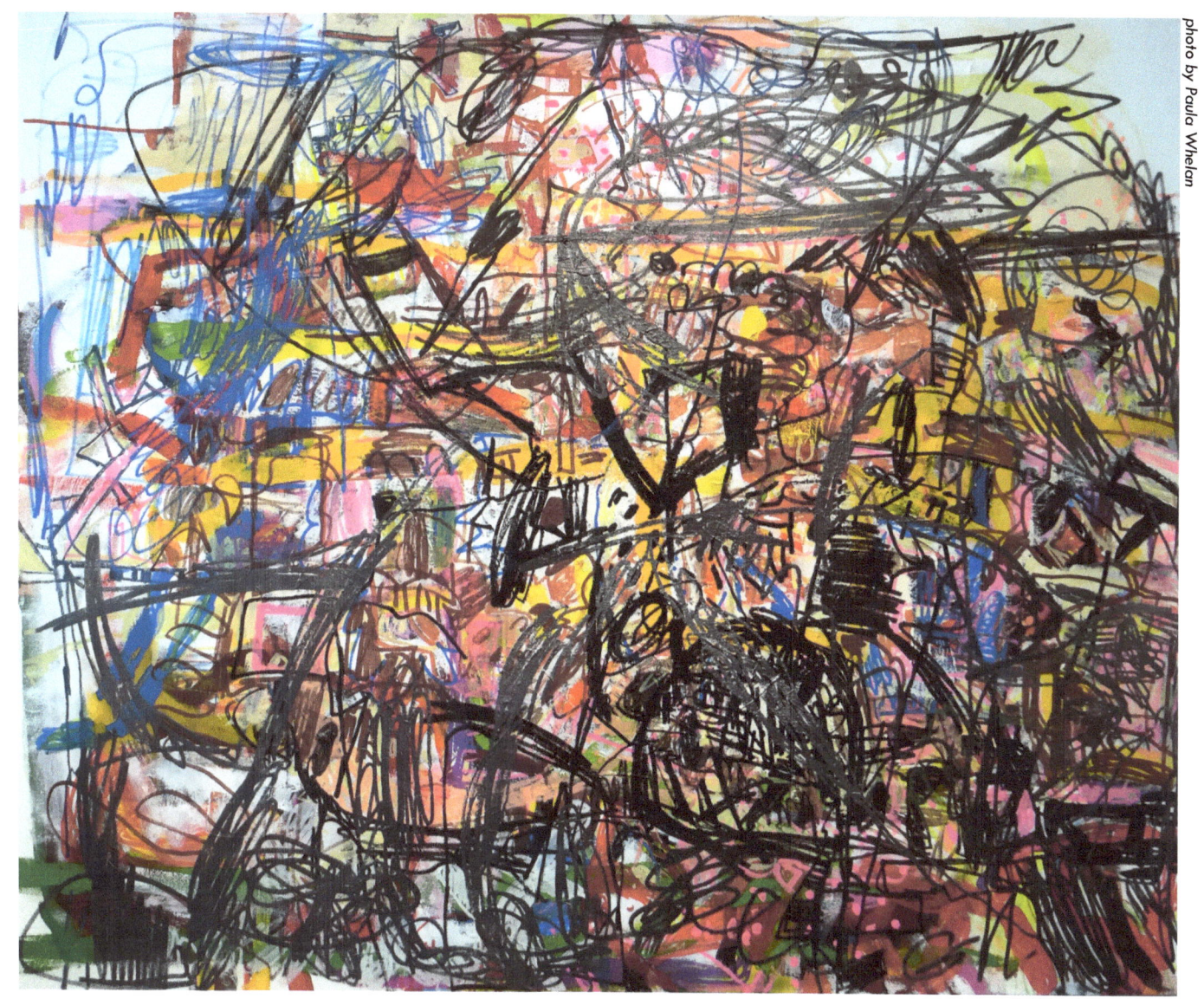

Indecisive
Mixed media on canvas, 42 x 52", 2018

Kate Vrijmoet

Biography

Painter, curator and social practice artist Kate Vrijmoet received her MFA from Syracuse University. Her paintings and installations focus on issues of consciousness, privilege, access and scale.

Working in both paint and social sculpture, Seattle artist Kate Vrijmoet uses the tools of classical painting to create high-impact experiences for her audience — experiences associated more with theatre. She is known best for both her large-scale water paintings and her life paintings, The Accident Painting series.

The social sculpture she creates are real-time exchanges between people to heighten consciousness with ourselves and others. "My role is to facilitate deep connections among us through art. In my work I am engaged in a highly energetic conversation with my audience and reflect that in the way I capture my subjects — deconstructing the figure, and finding rhythm in form."

Vrijmoet was one of 16 American artists participating in the 2012 5th Beijing International Biennial. Vrijmoet has exhibited in shows juried by curators of the MOMA (Paulina Pobocha), the Met (Anne Strauss), the Guggenheim (Nat Trotman), and the Brooklyn Museum of Art (Charlotta Kotik). She received a top Prize in 2010 Ecuador Biennial. Her work has been published in the books Creative Practices for Visual Artists by Kenneth Steinbach, and Ufora, New American Paintings, The Seattle Times, Catapult Magazine and Professional Artist Magazine, as well as in numerous catalogs including her CoCA Seattle solo exhibit catalog: Kate Vrijmoet: Essential Gestures, Uforafest, The Richard Siken Project, CoCA Annual 2014, and more. She has received several Grants. Vrijmoet is the creator of The Incredible Intensity of Just Being Human, an art & social change exhibit examining the stigma and silence surrounding mental illness.

Vrijmoet has curated, and facilitated multiple exhibits for Center on Contemporary Art (CoCA) while she served on the board of CoCA from 2016-2018 and as Board Chair in 2017-2018: Art n Math, and Painters Who Fucking Know How to Paint. In 2018, Vrijmoet served on a Community Incubator Team (Think Tank) with other community leaders and electeds who convened to work on the creation of a more sustainable arts culture in the PNW. Vrijmoet completed a 2-year certificate program in the principles of adaptive leadership through Leadership Eastside from Saybrook University in 2018. www.katevrijmoet.com

Acknowledgements

Several years ago Kate Sweeney bounded into my Pioneer Square Studio on First Thursday Art Walk and announced, "I'm going to curate a show called Painters Who Fucking Know How to Paint and I want you in it." Well... swoon.

We had difficulty finding a venue. But then I joined the board of the Center on Contemporary Art-Seattle, who embraced the idea enthusiastically. Three years later, here we are. I am not in the show, I am proudly co-curating it with the vigorous and abundantly talented Kate Sweeney.

We approached our curatorial task with excitement and a list minimally 100-artists-deep for our 650 square foot gallery space. While a joy to have reinforced, at least for myself, that painting is not an anachronistic endeavor, it was somewhat painful to cull the list to a mere 24 artists. To further narrow our list, Kate and I gave each other veto power over three of the other curator's choices and sovereignty to take back one vetoed choice, an act of trust and camaraderie for both of us.

I want to thank Kate Sweeney for a) having this fucking awesome inspiration for a show, and b) inviting me to play a key role in the creation of the exhibit. It's been an honor. Thanks to CoCA for providing support and personnel resources to this exhibit. Thank you Ray C. Freeman III for designing and publishing the exhibit catalog. Thank you to my outstanding intern, John Bellew, and all of your hard work, superb mind, and innovative ideas.

Thank you Elatia Harris, Nicole Francois, Wendy and Erik Heipt, Chloe and Xyta Vrijmoet and my husband, John Vrijmoet.

And thank you to painters, both in and out of this exhibit, for continuing to make fucking exciting work! Please don't fucking stop.

Kate Sweeney

Biography

A love of science and art led Kate Sweeney to receive a BFA, and then MFA in Medical Illustration from the University of Michigan. Scientific inquiry directs her work. The mind's idea of the world, macro and micro, fascinates her.

Kate maintains a fine art practice that is now centered on public commissions. She has been awarded commissions by Seattle City Light, Seattle Sound Transit, Washington State Arts Commission, Overlake Hospital and Facebook. She has had the pleasure of working with The Office of Arts and Culture and 4Culture, and has been honored to be a selection panel member. Her work is included in public, private and museum collections throughout the US.

Kate also continues to work as a medical and scientific illustrator. Her clients include surgeons, clinicians, medical researchers, and large environmental remediation projects.

"Everything I create seems to be influenced by some branch of science: quantum physics, medicine, natural phenomena. I love to take a scientific premise as a guiding principal to organize my images. It could be cloud chamber images from particle physics, old anatomy texts, mathematical patterns, the concept of dark matter, electron wave forms — anything that has an underlying pattern made by nature and divined by us through math. I then filter the concept through my sensibilities and create a world of rich color and rhythmic, dynamic, spatial juxtapositions. My work is inspired by science, but I balance an intellectual approach with exuberant color and energetic form to explore the fundamental energy underlying nature.

I seem to try a new medium with each body of work. My typical working method combines printmaking, digital techniques and various painting media. I examine analog versus digital aesthetics using a combination of techniques. I don't think in rectangles, but shapes. The free edge excites me. Like cave paintings, there are no borders, so form can move into the surrounding space."

Acknowledgements

It has been a pleasure to be able to work with the amazingly capable people at CoCA, a Seattle treasure. I am honored to have this opportunity.

Nichole DeMent is a stalwart champion of artists, and a cool head amidst the fast action that is part of mounting a show. She has been supportive of this crazy idea from the beginning. Her good nature amidst the frequent use of the F word while preparing this exhibit has been a tonic to my soul.

The staff at CoCA is thorough, capable, on task and prompt, to an amazing degree. I thank each of them.

Ray C. Freeman III has created a beautiful catalogue. I appreciate his dedication, patience and good nature.

Kate Vrijmoet is a force of nature who grabs hold of the tasks at hand and makes damn sure things get done just right. I have learned a lot from her.

And I am delighted and humbled by the artists in this show. I was so thrilled each time an artist agreed to participate that I would let out a hoop and a holler every time they sent in a 'yes'. They are all topnotch investigators into what can be a painting today. This is arduous labor, with an uncertain reward, and yet they persist. I am awed by the quality of their work and delighted with the selection we have gathered to share.

CoCA Publications

CoCA Exhibition Catalogs:

Heaven & Earth at Carkeek Park
Heaven & Earth I
Heaven & Earth II / Overgrowth & Understory
Heaven & Earth III: Cycles of Return
Heaven & Earth IV: Rootbound
Heaven & Earth 5: Acclimatized
Heaven & Earth VI: As Above. So Below.

CoCA Annual
CoCA 2009 Annual
CoCA 2010 Annual: Memory Upgrade
CoCA 2011 Annual
CoCA 2012 Annual
CoCA 2014 Annual: PostGlamism

Across the Divide
Across the Divide: Contemporary Art from the Scablands and Beyond
Across the Divide 2: Contemporary Art from Big Sky Country
Across the Divide IV: The New Boondocks

CoCA Members' Show
CoCA 2012 Members' Show: Show us Yours
CoCA 2013 Members' Show: Past, Present, and Future
CoCA 2014 Members' Show: Who Are You?
CoCA 2016 Members' Show: 35 Live
CoCA 2017 Members' Show: Make America Create Again
CoCA 2018 Members' Show: Creativity Persists

Group Shows
2009 East | West Emerging Artist Exchange
Resident Alien: Local Artists from Europe and the Mediterranean
(Un)Sanctioned: 13 Pacific Northwest Contemporary Urban Artists
Alive, Dead: 28 Artists' Interpretations
Ceci N'est Pas Une Pipe: Contemporary Flameworking
Change-Seed: Hong Kong and Beyond
Pop-Up (AR)t: An Atugmented Reality Pop-Up Book
JuarezX: Dragged Across Borders
Art n Math: The Intersection of Art and Math

Solo Shows
Kate Vrijmoet: Essential Gestures
Joseph Gregory Rossano: Whitewashed
Peppé: Limb from Limb
Gideon Kramer: Becoming

Blank Books:

CoCA Sketchbook 1
CoCA Gridbook

Occasional Monographs:

1 Otherwise This Stone
   Poetry by David Francis

2 Field Notes from the Chimalapa Wilderness
   David Francis

3 The Stars are Made from Love & Beauty
   An Introduction to the Journals of Joe Reno

4 A Morsel of Bread, A Knife
   Poetry by Roberta Feins

Curated Publications:

The Siken Collaborations
   *with Copper Canyon Press,
   curated by Joseph C. Roberts*

Heaven & Earth VII: Propagation
   with Center for Environmental Art

Calvet + Carbajal: Beyond Brut
   *with Frederick Holmes Gallery
   curated by Joseph C. Roberts*

Perseus II
   Miguel Edwards

In 2009, CoCA initiated the current publication series as part of our ongoing campaign to extend our activities outside the walls of the conventional gallery space and into the public realm.

These books make the exhibitions that we put on in our galleries and elsewhere accessible to a larger audience over a longer period of time that the lifetime of the actual show, and in a more physical, tactile form than the images on our website.

CoCA publications can be found at lulu.com/cocaseattle

www.ingramcontent.com/pod-product-compliance
Lightning Source LLC
Chambersburg PA
CBHW050803180526
45159CB00004B/1532